W9-BHQ-980

Praise for *The New Atheist Crusaders*

A snappy, yet serious tale of what intelligent faith means and how to keep it in your heart during these polarized times.

—Joan Roughgarden, Professor of Biological Sciences and of Geophysics at Stanford University and author of *Evolution and Christian Faith*.

Garrison scores what could be devastating points against the New Atheists.

—*Publishers Weekly*

I just finished reading *The New Atheist Crusaders* by Becky Garrison, and I don't know which is more genius, her substance or style. It is an enlightening read as it unpacks and exposes the flaws of today's pop-atheists with a brilliant, honest, and often hilarious writing voice. I have not enjoyed reading a book more than *The New Atheist Crusaders* in a very long time. Becky Garrison answers the atheists' objections to the shortcomings of religion by offering a hopeful vision of ordinary and imperfect people seeking to live in the way of Jesus. Trust me, this is going to be a book everyone is talking about, and for good reason!

—Jim Palmer, author of *Divine Nobodies* and *Wide Open Spaces*

Sassy, smart, and hysterically uncompromising, Garrison calls atheists and evangelicals to a deeper dialogue that moves beyond the aggressive self-righteousness of crusaders in all their guises.

—Shane Claiborne, activist, new monastic, and author of *The Irresistible Revolution*.

Finally we have an answer to moaning atheists—a credible, intelligent, and dynamic rebuttal to the woes of our society. Well written, reasonably argued, and full of insight. A book well worth reading for a modern age, and a must for anyone wanting to have a better understanding of the zeitgeist of life. Watch out Dawkins, Becky Garrison kicks butt!

—G. P. Taylor, *New York Times* best-selling author of the Shadowmancer series.

Even though Becky Garrison has earned a reputation as a gutsy religious satirist, and even though she puts the full force of her sharp skills to use in this exposé on the "new atheist crusaders," there is more going on here than you might imagine. Yes, she pokes good clean fun at their bloomers and fruit-of-the-loomers, but there are surprising confessional moments too, passages in which her vulnerability and humanity (can I say sincerity?) puncture the pretensions of her targets better than any direct confrontation. You'll get more than you bargained for in this book. A lesson in style and strategy as well as substance and content—I highly recommended it.

—Brian D. McLaren, author of *The Secret Message of Jesus* and *Everything Must Change* (brianmclaren.net)

THE NEW ATHEIST CRUSADERS

AND THEIR UNHOLY GRAIL

THE NEW ATHEIST CRUSADERS

AND THEIR UNHOLY GRAIL:
THE MISGUIDED QUEST
TO DESTROY YOUR FAITH

BY BECKY GARRISON

THOMAS NELSON
Since 1798

NASHVILLE   DALLAS   MEXICO CITY   RIO DE JANEIRO   BEIJING

Published in Nashville, Tennessee, by Thomas Nelson. Thomas Nelson is a trademark of Thomas Nelson, Inc.

Thomas Nelson books may be purchased in bulk for educational, business, fund-raising, or sales promotional use. For information, please e-mail SpecialMarkets@ThomasNelson.com.

All Scripture quotations are taken from The New King James Version. © 1982 by Thomas Nelson, Inc. Used by permission. All rights reserved.

Editorial Staff: Greg Daniel, acquisition editor; and Thom Chittom, managing editor
Cover Design: John Hamilton
Page Design: Casey Hooper

Library of Congress Cataloging-in-Publication Data
Garrison, Becky, 1961–
    The new atheist crusaders and their unholy grail: their misguided quest to destroy your faith / by Becky Garrison.
        p. cm.
    Includes bibliographical references and index.
    ISBN: 978-0-8499-1972-5 (softcover)
    1. Atheism. 2. Atheists. 3. Apologetics. I. Title.
    BL2747.3.G37 2007
    239'.7—dc22   2007024153

Printed in the United States of America
07 08 09 10 RRD 5 4 3 2 1

This book is dedicated to
the infamous doubting apostle, Thomas.
I know he gets a bum rap for refusing
to believe without seeing. But he teaches
me it's OK to question what's up with
God without losing the faith. Kewl.

CONTENTS

Contents

PREFACE

Rick Warren: Why isn't atheism more appealing
   if it's supposedly the most intellectually honest?
Sam Harris: Frankly, it has a terrible PR campaign.
Rick Warren: [Laughs] It's not a matter of PR.[1]

When people look at the Church and see only impostors,
   they conclude that Jesus is an impostor.[2]
—MIKE YACONELLI

OUR GOOD LITERARY FRIEND AND DICTIONARY
diva Noah Webster describes satire as follows: *a literary work holding up human vices and follies to ridicule or scorn; or trenchant wit, irony, or sarcasm used to expose and discredit vice or folly.*[3] According to Robert Darden, senior editor of the *Wittenburg Door* (the world's pretty much only religious satire magazine):

> The purpose of religious humor and satire is to hold a mirror before the church. We're the little boy who shouts, "Yo! People! The emperor is buck nekkid!" Religious humor and satire is an old and honorable tradition, as practiced by everybody from Elijah to Jesus. Its primary goal is to point out—in a

humorous way—hypocrisy and idol-worship among those who call themselves "religious," but who really seem to be more interested in furthering their own ends.[4]

In my position as senior contributing editor of the *Wittenburg Door*, I have become quite the spiritual sharpshooter as I hunt down sacred cows. While my focus has been smashing religious idols to smithereens, we now have these New Atheists peddling their misguided mess in the marketplace. Looks like I gotta adjust my scope and take aim at these ungodly gurus. Likewise, perhaps we as Christians need to pray about how our wayward ways might give these fools fodder. To that end, I'll try to honestly admit when we're wrong and call Christians (including myself) on the carpet as needed.

While it may appear to the casual observer that I am on a random hunting spree when I respond to their vitriolic venom with spiritual snark, my intent is to use the satirical format to get these secular scholars to look a little closer at themselves. This can be a lonely battle, for satire appears to be a lost art form in today's tense times.[5]

So then, as I respond to the cadre of claims made by these New Atheist crusaders in their best-selling books, you the reader need to understand that I do not claim, nor do I desire to claim, a position as an apologist. There are many talented theological types that can tackle that beast.

So, please don't take everything I say at face value. When fellow satirist Jonathan Swift penned *A Modest Proposal: For Preventing The Children of Poor People in Ireland from Being a Burden to Their Parents or Country, and for Making Them Beneficial to the Public* back in 1729, he never intended that the poor actually eat their own children as a means to alleviate poverty. Rather, as an Anglican clergyman living in Ireland, he employed his satirical skills to address the massive ills he saw before him. Likewise, while I make my statements with my tongue firmly implanted inside my cheek, buried beneath the literal text are golden grains of truth.

Like any pilgrim, I'm on a mission of sorts. I'm trained to go into the holy and hallowed halls of Christianity and sniff out religious rubbish. While everyone else sniffs their noses wondering what to do about that odious odor that's making everyone sick (spiritually speaking), I get to yell out, "This stinks!" Someone has to have the guts to come out and say what everyone else is thinking. It's a gift. It's a calling. In fact, one could say that satire is a spiritual discipline. While I have been called a "heretic" (and worse), I see myself as engaging on a holy quest in search of the radical and real Jesus. So let's begin our journey, shall we?

INTRODUCTION

Much of the appeal of today's popular
atheists—from Richard Dawkins to Sam
Harris—lies in the corruption of religion.[1]
—BRIAN MCLAREN

AS I EMBARKED ON MY FIRST PILGRIMAGE TO ISRAEL
in January 2007, my literary agent was negotiating the contract
for this book. When I checked my e-mail in Tiberius, I learned
from my agent that one piece of the puzzle was missing. I had to
come up with a snappy title lickety-split.

Suffice to say, viewing the arena where Jesus did the bulk of
His ministry while thinking of snarky ways to slam the anti-God
disciples represents a singular spiritual experience. Such is the
interior life of a religious satirist. As I surveyed the Sea of Galilee
from my vantage point on the Golan Heights, I uttered, "Richard
Dawkins, you are so wrong. God is not a delusion. No way. No
how. Instead, He's right here in the Holy Land."

If God was, say, Zeus, then He would have faded into the

1

pantheons of the imagination when the Jewish temple fell in AD 70 and pagan gods ruled the world. All that biz about coming down to earth as a man only to be crucified and then resurrected would have made for good bedtime reading, but nothing more. After all, museums display tributes to long-forgotten dead deities whose names hardly anyone in the twenty-first century can even pronounce.

Despite the debates over the exact place where Jesus of Nazareth was crucified, the specific church that marks the spot where Gabriel brought to Mary the Good News that would change the world, and other historical critical snafus, I seemed to feel the presence of God's saving grace throughout history every time I stepped on a piece of seemingly sacred soil. While New Atheists employ Greek gods, celestial teapots, and even vacuum cleaners to prove that God is but a figment of one's feeble and overactive imagination,[2] the recorded history etched into the fabric of the Holy Land clearly proves otherwise.

I am not a lone pilgrim searching for the real deal. The Pew Research Center for the People & the Press echoes this need for meaning-making in a post-9/11 world. According to their research, by a 51 to 28 percent margin, Americans think the lesson of September 11 is that there is too little, not too much, religion in the world.[3] This ongoing international discussion exploring what it means to be the church in the twenty-first century, the success of books such as Brian McLaren's *The Secret Message of Jesus* and Shane Claiborne's *The Irresistible Revolution*, coupled with the research for my book *Rising from the Ashes: Rethinking Church*,[4] indicates that our contemporary culture craves the spiritual.

Through my travels and travails covering this unique phenomenon called Americana Christianity, I've learned that many of those with a deep hunger to be fed spiritually are those souls for whom "church" is not in their vocabulary. Often they've been burned by one too many toxic church settings, or they grew up in a household where religion was either depicted as a system of rigorous rules or seen as inconsequential at best. These burnt buddies can embrace the universal message of Jesus, but they balk at how His teachings get corrupted by those prayer warriors who are engaging in some very public and tawdry theological battles in the religious-political arena.[5]

With so many people seeking spiritual solutions to our contemporary crises, how do we account for the recent rise of these New Atheists (aka "Brights"),[6] a group that tends to define the ideological conflict as being "between the Brights and the Dims, the Rationalists and Superstitious?"[7] In dishing their dirt, anti-God gurus Richard Dawkins, Sam Harris, and Daniel Dennett have succeeded in grabbing the media spotlight and the *New York Times* Best Seller List by ridiculing people of faith. What exactly is going on here?

> To those who suggest that religion is
> responsible for the ills of the world, the (French)
> Revolution offers an awkward anomaly.[8]
> —Alister McGrath

With the publication of *The Twilight of Atheism: The Rise and Fall of Disbelief in the Modern World* in 2004, one would think this whole God is Dead movement could finally rest in peace. After all, Alister McGrath, a molecular biologist and theologian, followed a path toward faith similar to that of fellow Oxford don C. S. Lewis. While these two former atheists may sympathize with seekers who choose to abandon a belief in God, they both employ their keen intellects to dissect fallacious teachings preached by practicing atheists.

According to McGrath, atheism's heyday began with the fall of the Bastille in 1789 and lasted until the fall of the Berlin Wall in 1989.[9] Throughout his book, McGrath takes the reader on a reflective journey of this brief but failed part in history, where atheism triumphed as the new religion of the state.[10]

While the French Revolution spawned its share of atheists, McGrath describes radical philosophers like Jean-Jacques Rousseau and Voltaire as Deists. Hence, they support an "ideal philosophical notion of God, based on reason or nature, rather than a more specifically Christian view of the matter."[11]

Now, one could scarcely call these French thinkers practicing Catholics. Clearly they considered themselves to be anti-church. And frankly, given the excesses of the era, who could blame them for taking such a negative view of all things religious? The gilded lifestyles enjoyed by America's most notorious televangelists pale in comparison to the lavish excesses that defined (and later doomed) the self-righteous reign of Louis XVI and Marie Antoinette. Not even Tammy Faye Bakker could bat an eyelash to Marie's makeup, and Jan Crouch's hair that praises Jesus pales in comparison to her highness's hairpieces.[12]

While we're at it, let's not forget the priestly perks that came with being a member of the high-ranking clergy. Had the *Wittenburg Door*, the satirical religious magazine for which I work, been around during this era, we would have had a blast until the powers that be sent us to the guillotine. (The editorial office gets more than its fair share of hate mail, but at least we all have our heads about us—literally.)

But were these philosophers also anti-God? New Atheists may select snippets such as Voltaire's infamous quote, "If God did not exist, it would have been necessary to invent him"[13] as demonstrable proof he hated God. But Voltaire also said that if you "eliminate the immortality, the power and corruption of the church, what reason for atheism remains?"[14]

Hmm. Now, given Voltaire isn't here to defend himself—and I refuse to dial up Miss Cleo or any other late-night TV psychic[15]—I propose that we file the "Do you believe in G-O-D?" question with all the other points we can ponder once we get to heaven and can see these famous folk face-to-face. But until then, I am not convinced that Voltaire is as anti-God as these rabid atheists perceive him to be.

In fact, Voltaire's critiques of French Catholicism's extravagant ecclesiological excesses, as well as its infectious role in corrupting the monarchy, bear an eerie similarity to the *Wittenburg Door*'s slams of the latest contemporary Christian scandal rather than a dude dissin' God. Speaking as the senior contributing editor for the nation's largest, oldest, and only religious satire magazine, I can attest that one can be a practicing Christian and still have some serious issues with the institutional church. Heck, I've been ranting against church crud since 1994, a good ten years before Harris hacked out *The End of Faith*.

A more subtle reading of philosophy during the Enlightenment reveals an ongoing tension between those who were attacking the powerful and questioning the creeds of a corrupt church, and rebels like Friedrich Nietzsche, who declared flat out that God is dead.[16] But *subtle* is not an adverb one employs when thinking about the moves Harris and Dawkins have made as they annihilate their opponents with all the tact of *Star Wars* stormtroopers.[17]

Still, religious movements ranging from Jesus freaks and megachurch mania, to, more recently, the emerging church, keep rising up to fill the spiritual void.[18] Despite the atheists' best attempts to relegate God to the sidelines or get Him kicked out of the game altogether, He keeps coming back to play ball. (I do get the sense, though, that God might like to score without any cheesy sports references praising His name in victory. But I digress.)

John D. Caputo, Thomas J. Watson Professor of Religion and Humanities and professor of philosophy at Syracuse University, notes, "A funny thing happened on the way to the funeral. The wheels came off the Enlightenment."[19] As modernity got kicked to the curb, McGrath reminds us how "while all religions have been affected in some way by the rise of postmodernity, its most significant casualty has been atheism itself."[20]

Been there. Done that. Next.

> The new atheism is too cut off from emotion,
> from intuition, and from a spirit of generosity
> toward those who see the world differently.[21]
> —Greg Epstein, Humanist Chaplain of Harvard University

But no. Instead, we're faced with yet another crop of atheist crusaders going off in search of the unholy grail. For those who need a scorecard, the New Atheist who started this whole public fracas is none other than media darling and pit bull Sam Harris (*The End of Faith: Religion, Terror and the Future of Reason* and *Letters to a Christian Nation*). Put a blonde wig and a too-tight black dress on him, and he could almost pass as an Ann Coulter act-alike. For Harris, 9/11 was the spark that started the fire that led to *The End of Faith*, while Coulter used this tragic day as a license to spew racist remarks.[22] Both are deplorable.

Leading the scientific brigade is the eight-hundred-pound evolutionary gorilla Richard Dawkins (*The God Delusion*), the stereotypical grumpy old man, who symbolizes the height of intellectual arrogance. He's right and you're not only wrong, but you're also a [insert the Dawkian insult of the day. Previous examples include linking the marking of children as "Jewish boy" or "Muslim child" as a child abuse,[23] observing how child-ish Christians suck on religion as if it's a dummy (pacifier),[24] and ridiculing people for using their faith like a celestial comfort blanket.][25] Dawkins gets miffed when this battle is called "19th-century" atheism, since, as he pontificates, "The period of their first discovery does not affect the truth of these propositions. But to call it '19th-century' is to draw attention to the important truth added in the 20th century: that religious belief persists in the face of these facts and arguments."[26]

Then there's Daniel Dennett (*Breaking the Spell: Religion as a Natural Phenomenon*), the Monty Pythonesque philosopher, a Bright who must be brilliant because no one can understand what he's talking about. Now, is it just me, or does he remind others of Donald Sutherland's portrayal of Professor Dave Jennings in *Animal House?*[27] Think about it: Dr. J's students thought they were all so cool and groovy getting stoned and blabbing on about useless philosophical constructs with the prof. But you gotta wonder once these kids aged a bit what they thought of his middle-aged tomfoolery.

Bringing up the rear, we have Christopher Hitchens (*God Is Not Great*) bellowing his way onto every conceivable cable TV show. This naughty English schoolboy loves to lambaste faithful followers who walk the walk, including Dietrich Bonhoeffer, Martin Luther King, and Mahatma Gandhi.[28] Yes, Hitchens can be hysterical, albeit in very small doses. But methinks he needs to check himself into religious rehab right about now 'cause he misses the mark far more often than he hits his target. I, for one, find if I get too high on my own hilarity, then I start to cross that fine line between satirizing my subject and slamming someone's soul. From all outward appearances, Hitchens staggered over that line a long, long time ago.

Moral indignation is a technique
to endow the idiot with dignity.[29]
—Marshall McLuhan

Now, given that Hitchens, Dawkins, Dennett, and Harris claim affiliations with Oxford, Tufts, and Stanford respectively, these four horsemen of the Atheist Apocalypse are no dumb dandies.[30] With their big bulging brains,[31] Charles Moore, editor of the *London Telegraph*, observes how they represent the mental equivalent of bronzed bodybuilders on the beach, kicking sand in the faces of us seven-stone (ninety-eight-pound) weaklings.[32] No one would dare accuse these guys of riding the little bus to school. No siree.

For reasons that escape me, these guys decry whenever a religious system claims to be a metanarrative, think "grand informing story," that embodies the one transcendent and universal truth. On the other hand, they have no problem applying metanarrative mojo to their own science-sensibilities. Do I detect the shuffling of some creepy test-tube fundamentalism?

So, lemme see if I get this straight. Those itinerant preachers who dismiss science with a few select Bible verses should be called on the carpet as backward buffoons. But it's A-OK for a New Atheist to trash anyone who dares differ with their viewpoints, even when there is disagreement within their own scientific community as to their conclusions. Huh? What gives here? Since when did these guys set the rules which we're all supposed to obey as if we're on some kind of an atheist autopilot?

This is all starting to remind me of my days under the PC-police when I was a student at Yale Divinity School (YDS).[33] This was back in the nineties, when political correctness careened into college campuses like some Stephen King-styled amusement park ride from hell. Back then, I was labeled "conservative" by allegedly more enlightened seminarians because I believed in the resurrection, liked to use male pronouns when talking about Jesus, and was one of the founders of the YDS Evangelical Fellowship. (This is why I laugh whenever I get called "liberal" because I contribute to the blog God's Politics.) I thought we'd all evolved to the point where we can dare to disagree without being dismissed with a derogatory sneer. But I can see it's clearly not the case.

At the very least, I would expect someone of Dawkins's caliber to employ the same scholarship to theology that he applies to evolutionary biology. But it seems this Oxford don tends to let his anger get the better of him, and then his critical thinking goes out the window.

When Terry Eagleton, professor of cultural theory in the Department of English and American Studies at the University of Manchester, reviewed *The God Delusion* in *The London Review of Books*, he remarked, "The more they detest religion, the more ill-informed their criticisms of it tend to be."[34]

In another review of *The God Delusion* in the *New York Review of Books*, H. Allen Orr, professor of biology at Rochester University, opines, "The most disappointing feature of *The God Delusion* is Dawkins' failure to engage religious thought in any serious way."[35] Here he outlines step-by-step where Dawkins misses the biblical boat. According to Orr, "you will find no serious examination of Christian or Jewish theology, no effort to appreciate the complex history of interaction between the Church and science, and no attempt to understand even the simplest of religious attitudes."[36]

For example, Dawkins's discernment skills seem to have taken a working vacation when he declared that *The God Who Wasn't There* (DVD) drivel represents "a sincere and moving film advocating atheism."[37] Come on. This pseudodocumentary pitted PhD-level atheists against Christians like the creator of Raptureletters.com. Talk about an unfair fight. How about I create a documentary defending the faith in which I put Rob Bell (aka Velvet Elvis) up against Tom Cruise? And to make it really fun, I can throw in a representative of the Worldwide Forgiveness Alliance, a member of the Worldwide Subud Association, and maybe even add the whole Kabbalah Center crowd for good measure. No contest. Bell would blow them all down.[38]

At least Dawkins admits that there are Christians out there who disagree with his views. When Dennett replied to Orr's review, he bragged that he only devoted a scant six pages of *Breaking the Spell* to the arguments for and against the existence of God. Apparently, he found almost all of the theological research on these topics to be "so dreadful that ignoring it completely seemed both the most charitable and most constructive policy."[39]

> Dennett climbs the highest peak of
> social science and victoriously raises
> the Darwinian flag, trying valiantly to
> ignore a herd of theologians sipping
> lattes in glacial caverns at the summit.[40]
> —David Marshall, *The Truth Behind the New Atheism*

How can anyone take seriously any analysis of religion that's penned by scholars who blow off such thinkers as Karl Barth, Jürgen Moltmann, and Walter Bruggeman? Wonder how Dawkins and Dennett would react if world-class theologians gave similar short thrift to their scientific treaties?

HOLDING CHRIST HOSTAGE

But why then are such books selling? Who's actually buying this stuff? Are we all so *American Idol*ed that we actually think nasty spiteful banter passes for informed intellectual discourse?[41] But more importantly, why have Christians allowed a few select secularists to hijack their faith and hold the teachings of Christ hostage?

When confronted with aggressive atheists, some Christians assume the mantle of the Cowardly Lion in *The Wizard of Oz* chanting, "I do believe, I do believe, I do believe," while lobbing biblical tracts and WWJD junk at these perceived lawbreaking infidels.[42] When are Christians going to learn that these aggressive tactics don't work? They turn everyone off, including those of us who actually try to practice the Christian faith. I stopped wearing my YDS sweatshirt because I kept getting bombarded by proselytizers asking me when I was going to "get saved" and enroll in a real Bible-based seminary.

Meanwhile, their progressive counterparts put everyone to sleep by droning on about "meaning making," "ecumenical partnerships," and "religious tolerance."[43] These spiritual squishes seem to forget that this "I'm OK, You're OK" touchy-feely gobbledygook went the way of 8-track tape players, mood rings, pet rocks, and other seventies-inspired inventions that offered instant satisfaction but proved to be abysmal failures in the long run.[44]

While conservative and liberal Christians offer ineffective means of coping with these attacks from the New Atheists, the pew sitters (aka the Silent Majority) resemble the three wise monkeys that "see no evil, hear no evil, speak no evil."[45] They operate under the naive assumption that by doing nothing all this controversy will simply go away and they can pray in peace.

Now, here I have a bit of a confession. I've been sitting on the fence hoping this fracas would just die down. After the beating I took from *Red and Blue God, Black and Blue Church*, I'm not exactly eager for another theological-political boxing match.

But these New Atheist dudes show no sign of extending the hand of compassion and mercy anytime soon. In March 2007 in

London, "leading British atheists squared off with defenders of the faith in a public debate on the motion, 'We'd be better off without religion.' Tickets cost nearly forty dollars, but so many people wanted to attend that the London-based event was moved to a bigger venue with over 2,000 seats. It still sold out. The audience declared the atheists the victors, by a margin of 1,205 to 778, with a few score abstentions."[46]

Alas, *Variety* reported in February 2007 that the Larry Charles and Bill Maher documentary on the topic premiered at the Berlin Film Festival. While promoting (aka "pimping") the flick to potential distributors, Charles billed this fare as "Bill Maher vs. the Antichrist (or is Bill Maher the Antichrist?)"[47] As long as people continue to buy into the anti-God game, this junk is gonna come down the pike. Time to put an end to this, once and for all.

So, I guess I gotta put on my satirical shorts, get into the ring, and put up my dukes.

There's the bell.

Round One.

HITCHENS FORFEITS FIGHT

WHILE READERS MAY HAVE WAITED EAGERLY FOR A ringside seat to witness a chick get into a bare-knuckled brawl with Christopher Hitchens, Twelve Publishers pulled their number one *New York Times* best-selling author out of the ring. Simply put, they refused to allow me to excerpt any material from *God Is Not Great.*[1] How anyone can publish a book filled with anti-God diatribes and then not allow the person who penned this poison to get into the ring and go the distance with a seasoned satirist remains a mystery.

Part of Warner Twelve's mission statement is to "seek to establish communities of conversation surrounding our books."[2] So, one would think they would come out swinging to see if this punch-drunk lightweight's arguments can withstand some spiritual yet satirical blows from the Christian corner.

Unfortunately, they seem to have cut themselves on Hitchens's beloved Occam's razor by concluding that the simplest and therefore best solution to this Christian confrontation is to throw in the towel and forfeit the match.[3] Yes, I clearly lack the necessary equipment or the salty vocabulary needed to go mano a mano with this unbiblical bully. That's too bad, because I was looking forward to drawing some of the sting out of his venom by showing how, in true Shakespearean form, *God Is Not Great* is but "a tale told by an idiot, full of sound and fury, signifying nothing."[4]

Fortunately Hitchens fails to make any substantial arguments not afforded by the other New Atheist Crusaders, so the battle can begin sans this delirious and dare I say delusional dude.

GOING GONZO
AGAINST GOD

If the universal search for God is so compelling,
what are we to make of those restless
hearts who deny his existence?[1]

—FRANCIS COLLINS,
DIRECTOR OF THE NATIONAL HUMAN GENOME RESEARCH INSTITUTE

FIRST OFF, LET ME MAKE CRYSTAL CLEAR THAT I DO not intend to convert hard-core atheists or their religious extremist counterparts. Like evolutionary biologist Joan Roughgarden, "I am concerned not with 'proving' whether or not God exists, but with living a Christian life."[2] Instead, my focus is on exploring how Christians can live out the teachings of Christ. Hence, I'm more concerned about ways we can open up the kingdom of God so that all may enter rather than setting up a coded system where fallen sinners have to go through a prescribed set of motions in order to win the ultimate all-you-can-pray salvation special.

Throughout my years at the *Wittenburg Door*, I've learned the hard way that those individuals who hold on to their beliefs with rock-solid assurance that they are right and I am horribly wrong cannot be swayed without some kind of divine intervention. Since I'm a follower of Christ and not a spokesperson for the Almighty, I will leave these souls alone in God's loving hands.

However, there's a key difference between arguing about the errors present in a particular religious tradition and saying that religion in and of itself is evil. These New Atheists aren't resurrecting the old atheist argument that belief in God is wrong. Rather, they're advocating that belief in God is dangerous and destructive. Furthermore, while old-school atheists came to the conclusion that God doesn't exist after some angst-ridden anxiety and serious soul-searching, this current crop of anti-God guys giggle like schoolgirls over their naughty refusal to kowtow to society and buy into this God biz.

If you don't want to believe in God, fine. But why can't these New Atheists give followers of the faith the right to believe in God if we so choose? I'd be happy to have us all play in our own respective spiritual sandboxes, except that religious extremists and now the New Atheists keep throwing sand in our faces.

Martin Marty, a church historian at the University of Chicago Divinity School, offers some sage counsel as he explores why we're in such an ideological quagmire these days:

> Fundamentalism is an expected reaction to the anomie that comes with social disorganization. When the social institutions become shaky, and uncertainty about the future becomes widespread, people look to religion to provide absolutes and a sense of security in the midst of their changing world.[3]

Looks like both New Atheists and their Christian counter-parts are grabbing onto their belief systems like Linus Van Pelt hanging onto his security blanket for dear life.[4] With all that's going on in the world, I get the need to hold onto something safe. But who ever said the Christian journey was safe and comfy? Ever since the late, great Mike Yaconelli edited my first article, "Beavis and Butthead Are Saved" and got me started on this whole weird world of serving God through my writing, "safe" is never a word I've used to describe my faith journey.[5] Scary, sweet, strange, sacrilegious, spiritual, yes. But safe? No way, no how. Never.

Even before I was a published writer, the Reverend James Annand, the former dean of Berkeley Divinity School at Yale, taught me the value of paying attention to my built-in BS detector. Simply put, he told us that whenever we're at any religious gathering and our devices start making noise, then we should pay attention 'cause something ain't right. Kewl. So that explains the buzzing sound that's been bugging me all these years. No wonder my brain hurt— too much heresy will do that to ya.[6]

Since graduating from YDS, my BS detector has been going into overdrive. At first, I thought I was having *Horton Hears a Who* moment.[7] Like the troubled Whos in Whoville, my inner voice just won't shut the heck up when something just ain't right. When I met Australian evangelist John Chapman back in the 1980s at a retreat,[8] he reminded our group how we need to discern if our inner rumblings are signs of the Holy Spirit or gas caused from eating a bit of bad cheese. Over the years, thanks to prayer and some discerning souls sent my way, I've come to realize that, no, I'm not crazy and hearing voices. Nor is my inner child throwing a temper tantrum. And if I have a stomachache, it's 'cause I ate too much religious rubbish. Simply put, I need to pay attention here, because when my gut starts acting up, something ain't right.

I'm not saying this is a "good thing," mind you. Ask Robert Darden, senior editor of the *Wittenburg Door*, what it's like to have to deal with me at times. It's not a pretty spiritual sight when I am convinced we have to shoot a particular sacred cow and he tells me to hold my horses, 'cause this particular cow ain't worth barbecuing. Having a big yap and a smarty-pants attitude carries with it some obvious and odious drawbacks for someone who tries to follow Jesus, believe me.

There are plenty of times when I've followed the way of Dawkins and Harris and let my anger rule the roost. Over the years, I've let words pass my lips that I wish I could take back, and it pains me that some self-proclaimed Christians won't forgive me for my past actions. Like these New Atheists, I can get myself so wound up in trying to prove a point that I miss the mark and come off as less than noble at best.

But let me try to see if I can keep my anger in check as I dissect the arguments made by those who are dissin' the faith. I've already dealt with the fanatical faithful who use religion for their own political and personal gain in *Red and Blue God, Black and Blue Church*. Now it's time to address this other group of strident souls who have no qualms about pulling rabbit punches and other below-the-belt moves in order to blast religion off the face of the earth.

THE NEW ATHEISTS' WAR ROOM

Common sense dictates that anyone declaring war would have some kind of an overall objective that can be implemented through a series of calculated actions. Former Secretary of State Colin Powell was right on the money when he observed, "When we go to war, we should have a purpose that our people understand and support."[9]

Now, here I admit I'm out of my league. Let's face it, I'm a religious satirist, not a military strategist. Sure I may shoot down people's sacred cows figuratively speaking, but I'm a real wuss when it comes to waging an actual blood, guts, and glory kinda war. But I do know enough to realize that I need to avail myself of the most up-to-date government-sanctioned documentation to help me analyze these atheists' militant actions. So I went to the White House's Web site and downloaded a copy of "Our National Strategy for Victory in Iraq."[10] Hey, don't laugh. I'm serious here. By the time my niece was six, she could beat me playing video games. I really have no clue about how a war room operates. I need all the help I can get.

Let's see. If I understand the credible contents of "Our National Strategy for Victory in Iraq," the powers that be tell me that in order to win a war, one needs to define what constitutes victory. Those in charge here tell me that victory in Iraq is defined in three stages—short term, medium term, and longer term. Oh, and victory in Iraq is a vital US interest. So it matters that the United States of America shoots and scores.

This document goes on to inform me that how the US

achieves this victory remains contingent on their strategy. As expected, they line out this strategy in a loose, step-by-step fashion. Their strategy for victory is clear, though it is (and must be) condition-based.

This clear (sic?) strategy appears to follow three broad tracks: the political track, the security track, and the economic track. Also, this strategy is integrated, and its elements are mutually reinforcing. And finally, while the US strategy is working, it will take time.

Got that? That's OK. Neither do I. But now at least I have a means of analyzing the New Atheists' campaign to wage war against the faith.

Once you start to examine their moves up close and personal, the New Atheists' war strategy appears to be flawed from the get-go. As confusing as this Iraq war plan might be, it seems to make far more sense than what these New Atheists seem to be plotting and planning. When I compare the US government's military strategy to the New Atheist's battle plan for victory over religion, my brain turns to Jell-O.[11] First off, I fail to see how they are defining victory. Yes, I know they want to "rid the world of all religion," but have they defined their victory in stages? Doesn't look to me like they've come up with any comprehensive anti-God evangelism campaign whatsoever.

Also, have they thought about whose interests are served if the world is rid of all things religious? *Newsweek* managing editor John Meacham reflects, "in the scientific world of the New Atheists, labs would replace cathedrals, brain scans, holy books. It would be different, but would it necessarily be better?"[12] Given I'm not much into having anything dictate my life, I'd prefer not to be controlled via machines or ministers. I guess no one bothered to tell these warmongers that their goal for a God-free world has been tried and has failed miserably as per the French Revolution, Stalin, and the list goes on and on and on. Heck, I can tick off secular examples of why ridding the world of religion doesn't work till the sacred cows come home.

But the New Atheists seem to turn a blind eye to atrocities committed under these totalitarian regimes. Keith Ward, professor of divinity at Gresham College–London, observes that "the two world wars were not fought on religious grounds at all. The reasons for them are complex but they largely involve the desire for territory, national pride and the aspiration to extend imperial control."[13] Rather than seeing historical tragedies through a more holistic viewpoint, the New Atheists prefer to hurl examples of abuses done against mankind in the name of God ad nauseum. Kinda reminds me of monkeys revolting in the zoo by flinging their food (and worse). As my Southern granny used to say, "Oh, Lordy. What a mess."

Maybe making sweeping statements without anything to back up one's assertions is just one of those PhD-level alpha male things that us chicks aren't supposed to understand. Whenever a group of guys start engaging in hard-core debates that inevitably end up with a massive outbreak of urinesis, I don my foul weather gear and get the heck outta there.

Here's where I get confused. When these "No Heaven. No Hell. Just Science"[14] strident secularists wage war against any soul who dares profess belief in God, exactly what are they fighting for? The *Modern Humanist* notes, "We seem to be fighting for what we don't believe instead of fighting for what we do believe."[15] In fact, if they stopped screeching for a moment, they'd see that a lot of us religious folks share some of their sentiments. Many of us get angry at the moves pulled by self-proclaimed Christians such as Fred Phelps (God Hates Fags), Pat Robertson, and Ann Coulter.[16] Even many atheists seem to be getting tired of select atheists indiscriminately bashing all people of faith. James Wood confesses in *The New Republic* that while he reads reams of atheism-related material, "there is a limit to how many times one can stub one's toe on the thick idiocy of some mullah or pastor."[17]

Throughout his *Wired* article, Gary Wolfe warns his fellow lax agnostics, noncommittal nonbelievers, and vague deists that Dawkins, Harris, and Dennett demand that they enlist as foot soldiers in this war against faith.[18] Like it or not, they're all supposed to line up as enlisted soldiers ready and willing to fight the good anti-God fight.

Seems to me these New Atheists are trying to enlist foot soldiers from a group that's already chanting "Hell, no. We won't go!" So, unless they can institute an atheist draft of sorts, I'm wondering just how they plan to amass this mighty anti-God army that's going to join them in battle.

I have a really strong hunch no one wants to touch those patriot players and other neo-Nazi skinhead types who always seem to be in the mood to engage in some serious Christian crushing.[19] I suppose you could draft Marilyn Manson fans, but first you'd have to convince them to move out of their parents' basements and take the occasional shower.

But back to their battle plan. Let's look at their strategy. What tracks are they following? As far as I can tell, they're engaging in print, online, and television blitzes to promote their best-selling books. Three distinct tracks. Just like the White House's plan for Iraq. Good. At least they have some kind of plan. Given that they endorse each other's products, their strategy, at least on some level, is integrated and mutually reinforcing.

But does this serve the common good? I can see where this campaign might serve their personal needs, but what about the rest of humanity? After all, what's the point of war if you're worse off than when you started? The last thing I'd think these guys would want to do is to start another failed French Revolution.

The aggressive antagonism displayed on the part of the New Atheists has even their fellow atheists up in arms. While believe-nothings like American Atheists national spokesperson Dave Silverman agree with their positions, he laments that "when we take on the mission to convert, or even be intolerant, . . . we become LIKE those who have oppressed us in the past. Fighting fire with fire may be correct, but it is distasteful."[20]

These ungodly gurus seem to forget that other equality movements such as women's rights and gay politics kept the primary focus on civil legislation. Yes, there are some loose cannons in any movement for sociopolitical change, but the general gist in other campaigns for equality is focused on granting everyone equal civil rights under the law, and that's that. Nothing more, nothing less.

Sounds kinda similar to Voltaire's critiques of the pre-French Revolution Catholic Church. In fact, most atheists, agnostics, and skeptics that I talk with these days express grave concern that certain religious organizations want to impose their particular beliefs on them. If they were free to just "be," then they'd be quiet and happy to coexist alongside religious folks.

YOUR SCHOLARSHIP IS SLIPPING

Now, when it comes to the actual weapons that the New Atheists lob against their opponents, they seem to be shooting blanks. We've heard this all before, albeit in a more scholarly format. Orr observes, "*The God Delusion* certainly establishes that Dawkins has little new to offer. Its arguments are those of any bright student who has thumbed through Bertrand Russell's more popular books and who has, horrified, watched videos of holy rollers."[21]

In the *Wall Street Journal*, Sam Schulman sums up their scholarship (or the lack thereof): "Spend as much time as you like with a pile of the recent anti-religion books, but you won't encounter a single point you didn't hear in your freshman dormitory."[22] He adds that he cannot see within the New Atheists' simple-minded parody "what might have preoccupied great artists and thinkers like Homer, Milton, Michelangelo, Newton, and Spinoza—let alone Aquinas, Dr. Johnson, Kierkegaard, Goya, Cardinal Newman, Reinhold Niebuhr, or, for that matter, Albert Einstein."[23]

Philosopher Alvin Plantinga takes Schulman's comparative exercise one step further: "You might say that some of his [Dawkins's] forays into philosophy are at best sophomoric, but that would be unfair to sophomores; the fact is (grade inflation aside), many of his arguments would receive a failing grade in a sophomore philosophy class."[24] Ouch. That's gotta hurt big-time.

If memory serves me correctly, many of my collegiate conversations of a philosophical nature were held when most, if not all, of us were under the influence of a substance that would have resulted in our expulsion from Wake Forest University.[25] To quote Dean Vernon Wormer's words of warning in *Animal House*, "Fat, drunk, and stupid is no way to go through life." I dunno about you, but I like my liver and other vital organs, and I'd rather not subject myself to another round of college-level inebriated discourse. Life's too short.

But these New Atheists seem to be stuck in freshman mode, theologically speaking. Why do we have to do Bertrand Russell's whole tempest-in-a-teapot scenario again? This is, like, so 1952. Been there, done that.[26] And stop throwing the Flying Spaghetti Monster at us like you're a buncha schoolboys engaging in a cafeteria food fight.

For those of you who haven't been following this whole teaching-intelligent-design-versus-evolution-in-the-public-schools debate, the Flying Spaghetti Monster is a parody religion created by Oregon State University physics graduate student Bobby Henderson in 2005. In an open letter to the Kansas State Board of Education, Henderson professed his belief in this pasta deity and asked that the school board respect his religious convictions. In addition to teaching intelligent design, he insisted that Kansas public schools also be forced to teach the "Pastafarian" theory of evolution.[27]

Dorothy's right. I don't think we're in Kansas anymore.

Even James Wood admits that "belief in God is a good deal more reasonable than belief in the teapot, precisely because God cannot be reified, cannot be turned into a mere thing, and thus entices our approximations."[28] And these are your fellow atheists talking here, you know, the ones you're trying to enlist in your battle against us faithful folks. I fail to see where you've made your case that they should be drafted to fight your anti-God battles.

27

Another line of faulty thinking comes through when these New Atheists try to define "the enemy." For reasons that escape me, when these so called "Brights" choose to cite Christians, they tend to pick those religious nuts from the lunatic fringe that keep religious satirists like me in business. If Dawkins bothered to check the American religious radar every once in a while, he'd see that Pat Robertson has been pretty much pushed to the sidelines.[29]

> Imagine someone holding forth on
> biology whose only knowledge of the
> subject is the Book of British Birds, and
> you have a rough idea of what it feels like
> to read Richard Dawkins on theology.[30]
> —Terry Eagleton, London Review of Books

Then we have the matter of their biblical source material. Dawkins cites Ann Coulter's *Godless: The Church of Liberalism* and John Shelby Spong's *The Sins of Scripture* in his bibliography for *The God Delusion*.[31] Now, here's an intriguing SAT-style question:

```
Ann Coulter : Christianity ::

(A) Dr. James Dobson : Sponge Bob Square Pants

(B) The New Thought movement : common sense

(C) Marilyn Manson : Satanism

(D) Dick Cheney : gun control

(E) The Democratic Party : family values
```

The correct answer is C. Both Ann and Marilyn found a profitable way to utilize religion as a provocative tool to feed their cash cows. Ann appeals to the base instincts of her rabid followers that right makes (Christian) might. Conversely, Marilyn attracts the kids of control-freak parents who want to rebel from what can best be described as a rigid and repressive regime. I'll let the Satanists deal with Marilyn Manson, but please, do not interpret Coulter's trademark viciousness and venom as viable Christian virtues.[32]

When Dawkins claims that the difference between the gospels and *The Da Vinci Code* remains "that the gospels are ancient fiction while *The Da Vinci Code* is modern fiction,"[33] he demonstrates a pronounced inability to engage in either serious literary or biblical criticism. Tomes of scholarly research starting back with Josephus can quickly refute Dawkins's inaccurate assessment that "the historical evidence that Jesus claimed any sort of divine status is minimal."[34] While we can debate Christ's divinity with gusto, the historical and biblical evidence makes a pretty strong case that during the period He was alive, Jesus of Nazareth had a pretty durn clear idea why He thought He was put on this earth.[35]

And while we're talking about living and breathing beings, please show me one serious theologian that these guys have wrestled with who is still on this planet. Sam Harris cites Paul Tillich as the one theologian he thinks "gets it" when Tillich chides those who believe "an act of knowledge that has a low degree of evidence."[36] I don't know how to break the news to Harris, but I would suggest perhaps examining those theologians who have come along since Tillich talked. (Paul Tillich died in

1965.) Theology, like any other discipline, does evolve, though one would never know it from Harris's backward approach to this discipline.

For all their talk about backwoods believers, self-professed thinkers like Dawkins and Harris refute religion by quoting material penned by the likes of St. Thomas Aquinas, St. Anselm, and Voltaire. Using medieval and Enlightenment thinkers as your primary source material in today's postmodern world doesn't strike me as a very Bright move.

> There is no text more barbaric than the Old Testament of the Bible— books like Deuteronomy and Leviticus and Exodus. The Qur'an pales in comparison.[37]
> —Sam Harris

Sometimes I get the feeling these atheist guys do all their religious research by trolling the halls of the American Academy of Religion/Society for Biblical Literature's annual meeting, looking for the odd scraps of religious rubbish. The majority of those who participate in this annual meeting of religious academics represent serious, world-class biblical scholars and theologians who are grappling with how to interpret ancient scriptural texts in light of the twenty-first century. But instead of sitting in on their enlightening and engaging seminars, the New Atheists get their religious fix by listening to loopy lunacy like *Hopeful Instability: Queer Love and Divine Desire in Religious Tradition* or *Tantric Buddhism Through the Chinese Looking Glass*.[38] Using this logic, I could go to the International UFO Congress in search of "scientific" data.[39] Yeah, right. I guess you have to get tenure somehow.

What's even more senseless is the New Atheists' penchant for quoting self-appointed pseudoscholars as the real deal. I hate to be the bearer of bad news, but I can't think of a serious biblical scholar who would agree with Dawkins's assessment that Spong is a "nice example of a liberal bishop whose beliefs are so advanced as to be almost unrecognizable to the majority of those who call themselves Christians."[40] Huh? Bishop Spong denounced the Nicene Creed as "alien to the world in which he lives."[41] Guess he must have been taking a spiritual snooze when, during his ordination as bishop, Spong said he would "solemnly engage to conform to the doctrine, discipline, and worship of the Episcopal Church."[42]

Alvin Plantinga speculates, "Could it be that [Dawkins's] mother, while carrying him, was frightened by an Anglican clergyman on the rampage?"[43] Henry VIII, the late Bishop James Pike of San Francisco, and yes, Richard Dawkins, represent a few prime examples of what can happen when Anglicans try to apply this whole Scripture, tradition, and reason three-legged-stool thingy.[44] Sometimes the stool breaks under the weight of human folly.

Like Dawkins, I, too, am part of the Anglican Communion. As a PK (preacher's kid), I OD'd on all the silliness and stuffiness that too often characterize the Frozen Chosen. Yeah, the church can terrify the bejesus out of us and make us quiver in our boots or walk away shaking our heads in disgust. Heck, my dad died a broken-down alcoholic, abandoned by both the Episcopal Church and almost all of the academic community. The letters and e-mails we get at the *Wittenburg Door* from people whose souls have been stained, thanks to religious organizations, break my heart. The institutional church can be toxic, no question about it. But just 'cause the church's teachings can backfire big-time doesn't mean God goes up in smoke as well.

Still, I can see the appeal of Spong-styled scholars, religious relics, and psychotic pastors to a rabid New Atheist. Rather than examine the full range of theological scholarship, why not just pick and choose those quotes that will justify one's preconceived bias against all people of faith? Guess that explains why this latest barrage of anti-God New York Times best sellers might be full of sound and fury, but in the end, they signify nothing new.

In fact there appears to be some disagreement among these anti-God gurus regarding what even constitutes an atheist. The *Merriam-Webster Online Dictionary* defines "atheism" as "1) a disbelief in the existence of deity or 2) the doctrine that there is no deity."[45]

Daniel Dennett declares, "We Brights don't believe in ghosts or elves or the Easter Bunny—or God"[46] According to Sam Harris, "Atheism is nothing more than the noises reasonable people make when in the presence of religious dogma."[47] (Using this illogic, I, too, could be an atheist, because the job of a religious satirist is to rant and rail against devilish dogma.) Dawkins's preferred source of biblical authority, Bishop Spong, takes a more loosely defined view of the word *atheist*, pontificating that "this word for starters does not mean, as people commonly assume, one who asserts that there is no such thing as God. It means, rather, that one rejects the theistic definition of God."[48]

If the no-god gang can't even agree on what it means to be an atheist, then why are they railing on people of faith? Wouldn't it make more sense for these guys to figure out within their own atheist camp what they don't believe before bugging the rest of us?

Along these lines, Christians who use terms like "atheist" to denigrate those who don't adhere to their specific set of beliefs should bone up a bit on their church history. As Stephen Tomkins observes, "Christians were called atheists by the Romans because Christians denied the gods, refused to sacrifice to them for the good of the community, and shunned city feasts."[49] Spong suggests having a sit-down between the two parties. If Christians refuse to sit down and have a reasoned discussion, "that is a tip-off that the God they serve is in fact an idol, and atheism is always a proper response to idolatry."[50]

While I'm all for dialogue over diatribes, it looks like once again, Spong appears to be twisting the Bible a bit to suit his own agenda. Wouldn't the response to idolatry be the authentic living out of one's faith tradition instead of choosing not to believe at all? Also, in his ongoing quest to damn institutional Christianity, Spong seems to conclude that believers are the only ones being belligerent here. But once again, it's easier to point fingers at those one despises than try to work toward bringing disparate voices together.

Conversely, can we have a moratorium on passing off "Jesus said it; I believe it; that settles it" catchphrase Christianity as serious scholarly discourse? A *Newsweek* poll conducted in March 2007 concluded that 91 percent of American adults say they believe in God, and 82 percent identify themselves as Christians.[51] However, when I observe how Stephen Prothero, author of *Religious Literacy*, documents our descent into religious ignorance,

I gotta confess that as a country we don't know spiritual squat when it comes to articulating the basic tenets of the Christian faith, not to mention our abysmal ignorance about other religions.[52]

If we Christians accept the Word of God on blind faith without wrestling with the biblical text and reflecting on centuries of commentary, then how can we expect these New Atheists to do likewise? When we present shallow scholarship, we should be ridiculed. End of story.

Not to worry, when I refute the New Atheists' shoddy scholarship, I'm not about to do a postmodernist "Do Derrida, Do" rant, leap over Lyotard, or start flashing Foucault. I'm a religious satirist, not a theologian or a philosopher. Hence, I know my limits, so I'm not going to venture onto turf where I know full well I lack the necessary street cred.[53]

But I would challenge these New Atheists to lay down their theological and spiritual smack[54] and go mano a mano with postmodern thinkers like Brian McLaren, John D. Caputo, or N. T. Wright. No contest. In the end, those spiritual seekers who are moving forward would triumph over the dead delusionals living in the past.

> The kingdom of God is not simply a new
> belief or doctrine that can be patched
> into an old way of life; it is; rather, a
> new way of life that changes everything.[55]
> —Brian McLaren

Sorry, but New Atheists have gotta do better than trash-talking their opponents. Such maneuvers will get you press, but then so does flashing the paparazzi, shaving your head after a bender, and yelling anti-Semitic phrases while being pulled over for a DUI. When I checked the *New York Times* best seller list back in March 2007, alongside Dawkins and Harris were literary giants (*sic?*) Bill O'Reilly, Dr. Laura, and Rhonda Bryne (*The Secret*). Guess this all proves that just because you can get media attention doesn't mean you have anything meaningful to say.

Show us the money or go home . . . Next!

> Now that I am a Christian I do have moods in
> which the whole thing looks improbable; but
> when I was an atheist I had moods in which
> Christianity looked terribly probable.[56]
> —C. S. Lewis

Thinkers like Richard Dawkins hold that, while materialism is based on painstaking research and rational thought, religious views are based on 'blind faith' some sort of leap in the dark, and so are painstakingly irrational and unthinking. Since ignorance is morally reprehensible, religious belief is not only based on falsehood and deceit, it is morally wrong.

What are we to say about this? Has Dawkins never read any philosophy? Is he not aware of the weaknesses of materialism? Is he not aware that the philosophy of common sense espoused by his favorite philosopher, David Hume, has been pretty comprehensively undermined by science? Or that Hume himself could never reconcile his commitment to skeptical reasoning, which undermined belief in casual laws and other persons as well as God with his common sense beliefs? Does he really think that Descartes, Leibniz, Spinoza, Kant and Hegel were all unthinking simpletons? I believe that any reasonable person, faced with all the wide array of philosophical arguments throughout history and today, would be forced to admit that no worldview (no system of metaphysics) has gained universal consent among the informed peer group of professional philosophers.[57]

—Keith Ward, *Is Religion Dangerous?*

DOES GOD MATTER?

All men need the gods.
—HOMER, CA. 800 BC

A certain portion of mankind do not believe
at all in the existence of the gods.
—PLATO, CA. 400 BC

If God created the universe as a
special place for humanity, he seems to have
wasted an awfully large amount of space
where humanity will never make an appearance.[1]
—VICTOR STENGER

HERE'S WHAT I DON'T GET. IF SOMEONE THINKS there is no being called God, then why are they throwing these anti-God temper tantrums? Why rail against what they perceive to be a nonexistent being? Doesn't that represent an unscientific response here?

I don't believe in the goddess Sophia, Zeus, or Madonna (the rock star, not the mother of Jesus). So I don't even bother foot-noting items I think are nothing more than nefarious nonsense. Furthermore, I tend to ignore people who babble on about their worship of said beings. If they go public, as did Shirley MacLaine, about their flaky flights of fancy, I'm liable to poke fun at them in the *Wittenburg Door*. But it's all in good-natured fun. No harm done. But these guys mean serious business!

Let's take their need for concrete data to prove that God exists. One of their common laments seems to be that if God existed, he'd just show up and settle the score once and for all. Victor Stenger echoes the demand stated by his fellow academic atheists: "A God who provides humans with important knowledge that they cannot obtain by material means should have produced testable evidence for his existence by now."[2] They seem to act as though God is a genie in a biblical bottle, always willing and eager to please. Every time a true blue believer rubs the magic lamp and says the perfect praise phrase, God'll just pop out and give his best Robin Williams impersonation. Get real. Once again, they've depicted a cartoon caricature of Christianity, not the real deal.

Maybe this has to do with their upbringing. From what I've read, these New Atheists tend not to come from what one would describe as religious households. Well, neither did I, for that matter. From a very early age, I was taught an unhealthy irreverence for both religious and academic authority figures. My admittedly eclectic religious education consisted of my late father, the Reverend Dr. Karl C. Garrison Jr., explaining to me the catechism of the Episcopal Church, as well as the meanings behind the lyrics to "Plastic Jesus," "The Vatican Rag," and "Wolfgang Amadeus Mozart Was a Dirty Old Man."[3] While my father made the inaccurate assertion that he introduced Timothy Leary to LSD, I charted the timeline of these two esoteric thinkers' respective lives. Looks like there were a couple of times they definitely could have hooked up and gotten high. And maybe Dad introduced him to some other psychedelic substance. Who knows?

Look, I get the New Atheists' need to buck authority, because I've been taught to do that for as long as I can remember. But there's a line between asking probing and satirical questions and just being pompous and silly. H. Allen Orr is right on when he complains how "Dawkins spends too much time on what can only be described as intellectual banalities."[4]

Like Dawkins, Stenger appears to be obsessed with the need for concrete proof that the Son of God was a real man. He feels that if Jesus of Nazareth really walked on the earth, someone would have unearthed His actual bones.[5]

At the risk of sounding like a really bad pseudodocumentary, let me try to explain why this quest makes no sense. I don't want to get medieval here, but frankly, how many Christians in the twenty-first century need the bones of Jesus as proof of their faith? After all, according to the resurrection story, Christ transcended matter. If you read the Gospels (hint, hint), you'll discover that Mary Magdalene found an empty tomb, not a body.[6]

Also, look at the Easter story in its proper sociopolitical context for a sec. Right about now, Jesus and His crowd were persona non grata (mild understatement). The so-called leader of this ragtag group of rabble rousers had just been crucified. Unless Jesus rose from the dead, all their years of following Him would have been for naught. Before they encountered Him on the road to Emmaus,[7] they had no clue if Jesus was the real deal, or if they had just drunk the wrong Kool-Aid by following a false prophet. They were left leaderless and scared for their lives, knowing full well they might be next on Pontius Pilate's hit list. Suffice to say, tensions were running pretty durn high.

As expected, the Romans did everything in their earthly power to prevent this resurrection myth from developing legs. The tomb was sealed, and guards were posted outside the cave 24/7.[8] No way they would have let the disciples steal the body and run around claiming that Christ had risen. No siree. From a historical standpoint, the resurrection story could not have occurred without some kind of divine intervention. Check out a timeline of the early church and it's pretty clear that saying you believed in the risen Christ was a deadly move.[9] Why would so many people risk banishment, torture, and even death for such an elusive myth?

Fare such as *The Lost Tomb of Jesus* tries to offer archeological proof that two stone ossuaries contain the remains of Jesus and Mary Magdalene.[10] But the evidence presented in this film remains shaky at best, according to credible archeologists. Just circular file this pseudodocumentary along with homegrown UFO video footage, JFK conspiracy crud, and other unsubstantiated, fanciful flicks that are so foolish they don't warrant any footnotes. Museums are littered with the remains of ancient kings who received a royal burial. If you read the biblical story, you'll see that Jesus was crucified like a common criminal.[11] Also, He made it pretty clear that His kingdom was not of this world.[12] Hence, Jesus of Nazareth would not have been entitled to a royal burial that would ensure His remains would be preserved for centuries to come.

Once again, boys and girls, using empirical data to describe a transcendent God that defies human descriptions doesn't work. 'Nuf said.

> Atheism turns out to be too simple. If the
> whole universe has no meaning, we should
> never have found out that it has no meaning.[13]
>
> —C. S. Lewis

Dawkins attempts to engage in scientific meaning making through the use of a cultural replicator he terms "memes" (not to be confused with M&Ms, mmm-good or Auntie Mame).[14] According to Dawkins, a meme spreads from one brain to another brain, like a virus. Hence, one can become infested with religion as though faith was a contagious and deadly disease.

If you're confused, that's OK. Most other scientists don't seem to get it either. And they have far more training in this subject than most of us. Lewis Wolpert, a developmental biologist, states, "Just what a meme is and how it is distinguishable from beliefs, I find difficult."[15] Also, Orr sees "no difference between saying that my morals derive from, say, Christianity and saying that my brain hosts a 'Christian morality meme.'"[16]

In fact, except for Dennett, I'm hard-pressed to find fellow scientists who concur with Dawkins's insertion of memes to a discussion of religious beliefs. While this isn't a popularity contest per se, wouldn't the entire scientific community embrace wholeheartedly a discovery of this magnitude? You would think so. Nope. No way. No how.

Now, what does a meme look like, you may ask? Ah, there's the dilemma. See, you can't see a meme, just like you can't see

God. However, in the gospel according to Dawkins, his memes represent reality, whereas God is fiction. Wow. Dawkins's discovery is starting to sound like the stuff spewed by Dr. Mephisto, the mad geneticist on *South Park*.

Upon entering his worldview, you encounter bad memes and good memes. Think of this as akin to the good witches and bad witches in *The Wizard of Oz*. Like the flying monkeys, wizards, and talking scarecrows that populate the Land of Oz, similar flights of fancy abound in Dawkinsland.

I'm not exactly sure what constitutes "good memes," but Dawkins remains quite adamant that religion represents "bad memes." The problem with these bad memes is that they can infect the brain and render one unable to reason. Apparently, this mental virus gets transmitted to children via those adults that are already suffering from this dreaded devotional affliction.

Now, Dawkins must be some kind of a neat freak, because he seems to have a pathological need to get rid of bad memes and replace them with good memes. I'm still not clear what a world would look like if it were filled with nothing but Dawkins-style good memes. You could throw in a crowd of Disney puppets singing "It's a Small World," as adventurous atheists trek through Darwin's Jungleland. The weakest and smallest atheists could be seized and eaten by some kind of bulbous plastic dinosaur and then charged five bucks for the come-to-Darwin automatic photo. Add an interactive ride on the Atheist Adventure Express, and you've got your own Bright 'n' Barney theme park. Pass me the Pepto. This sounds about as dreadful as those Christian theme parks we keep spoofing in the *Wittenburg Door*.[17]

Does God Matter?

I think that there are no forces on this planet more dangerous to us all than the fanaticisms of fundamentalism, of all the species: Protestantism, Catholicism, Judaism, Islam, Hinduism, and Buddhism, as well as countless smaller infections.[18]

—Daniel Dennett

With an anti-religious, rigid mind-set that they must rid the world of God because faith represents an infection that needs to be eradicated, these New Atheists have no choice but to aggressively spread their message, much to the dismay of other atheists. As expected, in their rapid zeal to spread what they perceive as good news that will save mankind, they tend to come off as "mad scientists" with all the odious, obnoxious, and obtuse features that define those inerrant street evangelists who pester passersby with pamphlets.

Ungodly Standards

You know, I gotta wonder just what kind of data sheets they're handing out to their potential converts to prove God does not exist. Just how does one use earthy empirical standards of weights, measurements, and mathematical calculations to analyze God, who transcends time, space, and matter? You can't dissect God the same way you would a frog in biology class, where you cut open the parts and examine the bits one by one and then figure out how the multiple layers can constitute God.

Right about now, I could whip out my copy of Peter Rollins's

How (Not) to Speak of God and quote his postmodern take on this whole level-of-being biz.[19] Then, I could whack these dudes over the head with the complete works of Phyllis Tickle. This Southern scholar has written more than thirty books. So I know that pelting them with her prophetic prose would hurt like heck, both literally and figuratively.

While these moves might lend a novel perspective to the debate, it'd just bring me down to their level of intellectual discourse. 'Sides, what's the point? Dawkins will just diss these dudes, Locke, stock, and barrel.[20] Something tells me these New Atheists have never really wrestled with Christian theological titans. Rather, they just give their work a cursory glance and then denounce them as dead and dumb delusional dullards. Just call it a strong hunch.

Not being a scientist, I decided to consult the National Academy of Sciences (NAS) to get their input on how they address this whole science-faith dichotomy. After all, this group was signed into being by Abraham Lincoln on March 3, 1863, and counts more than two hundred Nobel prize winners among its 2,000 members and 360 foreign associations.[21] So, one would think that their words would carry some degree of street cred. Kewl.

Well, according to the NAS, "Science can say nothing about the supernatural. Whether God exists or not is a question about which science is neutral."[22] Sounds like the NAS supports my suggestion that we play in our own sandboxes without throwing sand at each other. So why are the New Atheists bucking the NAS? What gives, guys?

When Dawkins tries to claim that when Christians reference

"God," we might be referring to some deity worshipped by, say, Martians from outer space,[23] methinks he might be reading a few too many cheesy science fiction novels. I have yet to meet one sane soul who worships these said gods. Now, I could apply this loopy logic and infer that all scientists could follow the warped ways of, say, L. Ron Hubbard or Captain Kirk. But let's not and say we did.

So then, Victor Stenger joins Dawkins in firing more blanks. He tries to disprove God by stating that if such a life force [like a soul] exists [within us], then we should be able to detect its presence. Now, here's where their argument gets really loopy. You see, when Stenger uses the phrase "life forces," he's referring to chi (qi) and ESP, as well as the use of psychics and mediums to communicate with the dead. I kid you not.[24]

Look, just because some TV-friendly medium like John Edward claims he's crossing over doesn't mean he's right, or even sane for that matter. I have lost most of my immediate family, and hence my heart goes out to anyone who wants to reach out one last time and achieve some kind of closure. Both of my parents died suddenly when I was but a bratty teen, and I'd give just about anything for a chance to say "I love you." But I know these programs are shams. So far, I've kept my change and my sanity. But I've been awake at three in the morning, and I gotta admit, those crass infomercials can be mighty tempting on those days when you're down 'n' out.

Of course, many people want to believe badly enough that they'll fork over their hard-earned cash and all their earthly possessions for the off chance of an otherworldly encounter. Desperate people sometimes do desperate things. The *Wittenburg Door* gets letters all the time from people who've been duped by faithless scam artists, and now assume that anyone who believes in Christianity must be cut from a similar cloth.

I hate to admit it, but there's more than a grain of truth to these comments. I've been in enough church settings where everyone was too consumed with preserving their own personal piety to hear my pain. So I get this deep inner craving to seek out anything—be it book or bottle—that will provide temporary relief from what feels like the fires of hell.

The Christian community's lackadaisical, lukewarm, and at times ludicrous portrayal of the teaching of Jesus Christ gives these anti-God musclemen ample ammo to knock the faithful to the floor. Richard W. Fox illustrates in *Jesus in America* that there have been plenty of times when American Christians have behaved in ways that must have our Savior shaking His head.[25] Let's not relive the ridiculous hysteria that led to my ancestor, the Reverend Roger Williams, getting the boot out of Rhode Island,[26] discussions of evolution that keep de-evolving into monkey business lickety-split, and the televangelist buffoons with their pathetic pay-to-pray schemes.[27]

When dealing with those who use fallen Christians as onto-logical proof that God does not exist, Francis Collins reflects, "The pure, clean water of spiritual truth is placed in rusty containers." Then he offers a cautionary to those who would blame God for all the church's misdeeds. "The subsequent failings of the church down through the centuries should not be projected on to the faith itself, as if the water had been the problem."[28]

I would add to Collins's comments that as Christians, we still should do our best to hose down those false prophets who preach a gospel that's so watered down that Christ has been flushed away. Whenever we see one of these bedazzled buffoons parlaying their latest spiritual shtick through books, videos, and television shows, we should stand up and collectively kick that "Christian" charlatan to the curb. Then we should pick up the people they've deceived and show them the redemptive power of Christ's healing love. That's the power of *agape* love in action, a Christ-centered power that can never die. If we truly strive to be like Jesus Christ, that means we each seek to live a life of faith that, as Charks Moore muses, "governs the whole of life, indeed the whole existence of everything. It therefore matters not only how we reason, but how we feel, how we act towards others, how we speak, sing, dance, laugh, cry, eat and wash, how we die, how we pray and how we love."[29]

> The truth of Christianity is life.
> The implications of this are vast.[30]
> —Peter Rollins

When we turn to God via our rational faculties, we simultaneously recognize both the underlying rationality of our faith in God and yet also reason's insufficiency to grant us what we *really* long for: light itself in a dark world. That light, however, only comes from God, not reason. We are pilgrims, and reason is our viaticum—but it is only viaticum. The nourishment this food for the journey provides is salubrious (when the reasoning is correct), but it is not life itself, only the provisions for life, which only God can provide.[31]

—Edward T. Oakes, SJ, *First Things*

ALL FAITHFUL
AREN'T FOOLS

Religious dogmatism impedes medical research,
starts wars, diverts scarce material and intellectual
resources—in short, it gets people killed.[1]
—SAM HARRIS

IF ONE TAKES A BRIGHT VIEW OF THE WORLD,
humankind becomes divided into two categories: enlightened
atheists and faith-talking neanderthals. Church historian Stephen
Tomkins laments on the Ship of Fools Web site, "Rather than
surveying the countless varieties of religion, weighing up their
mixed record, and arguing that on balance we'd be better off
without it , he [Dawkins] is only willing to see the dark side, and
writes off the whole thing, dismissing evidence that makes a
monochrome worldview uncomfortable."[2] For these secular
souls, religion represents a black-and-white bogeyman hiding in
the historical closet. Be careful or else an imaginary god is gonna
come out at any moment and scare the living bejesus out of you.

I'm convinced that these guys are really closet Joe Bob

Briggs fans.[3] Their depictions of all Christians as bumbling, violent buffoons bear an eerie resemblance to the fare served up in cheesy Roger Corman flicks.[4] Both of these misrepresentations of reality present poorly drawn stock characters, razor-thin plot lines, and other such spiritual schlock. The difference, of course, is that Corman knows he's writing fiction. I have no clue what concoction the New Atheists think they're creating.

In *The God Delusion*, Dawkins devotes five pages to explain in graphic detail the dastardly mistreatment of Edgardo Mortara in the mid-nineteenth century.[5] Using prose that would make John Waters proud,[6] he explores how the evil Vatican kidnapped this Jewish boy and then forced him to be raised Catholic. Apparently the boy came from a loving Jewish home, so there was no reason to remove Edgardo from his parents and force him to grow up in an abusive environment courtesy of the Roman Catholic Church.

> No one expects the Spanish Inquisition.[7]
> —Monty Python

The Spanish Inquisition and Edgardo Mortara's abduction should serve as a warning to all evangelists how not to interpret the command in the gospel of Matthew that "this gospel of the kingdom will be preached in all the world as a witness to all the nations, and then the end will come."[8] These stories also remind us once again of the dangers that can occur when religion becomes welded to the state. When religious leaders dismiss violence done to others in the name of God with a dismissive, "Oops, sorry. That won't happen again. Too bad," the collective Christian community should rise up and go after them with gusto.

Canadian philosopher Charles Taylor hit the nail on the end when he pointed out how both parties share some of the blame in turning a blind eye to atrocities done throughout humanity. When atheists decry that all violence is caused by religion, what they're really expressing is something along these lines: "The terrible violence of the 20th century has nothing to do with right-thinking, rational enlightened people, like me. The argument is then joined by the other side by certain believers, who point out that Hitler, Stalin, Pol Pot, etc. were all enemies of religion, and feel that good Christians like me have no part in such horrors. This conveniently forgets the Crusades, the Inquisition, and much else."[9]

> The product of such zeal is often justified in the name of Christianity, but in reality, it has nothing to do with believing in Jesus Christ.[10]
> —William Wilberforce

Regrettably, the institution church has stood by silently as the Holocaust, Bosnia, and Rwanda unfolded before their eyes. While some church leaders are waking up and rallying behind Darfur,[11] I gotta confess that unless there's oil or the Holy Land at stake, the US institutional church by and large takes a collective snooze when it comes to addressing atrocities being done to others in the name of God. All too often we tend to forget that Jesus commanded, "Let the little children come to Me, and do not forbid them; for of such is the kingdom of God. Assuredly, I say to you, whoever does not receive the kingdom of God as a little child will by no means enter it."[12] Yet, according to UNICEF, thirty thousand children around the world die each day from largely preventable causes.[13]

With stats like that, I'm surprised we don't have more atheists. When I hear of Bibles being delivered where there's no bread to eat or medical equipment on hand, I have to wonder just how these missionaries interpret the miracles of the loaves and fishes, where Jesus fed everyone both spiritually and physically.[14] Along those lines, the Christian community must come up with a more reasoned response than "just say no" when confronted with so many children dying worldwide from AIDS and from complications related to the abuse of drugs and alcohol—all passed on to them by their parents. What in God's name are we doing to help them besides keeping trendy with whatever the latest Christian status symbols might be?

SMEAR CHRISTIANITY

Dawkins seems to take a rather perverse delight in exploiting the horrors done in the name of God ad infinitum. For example, he goes into elaborate detail in *The God Delusion* about New Destiny Christian Center's Senior Pastor Keenan Roberts's Hell House outreach ministry.[15] Dawkins even has the audacity to declare that this pastor is "mainstream in today's America."[16] Uh, I report on religion for a living, and trust me, this Roberts falls into the fringe category.

For those of you who don't scour the country looking for religious drek, let me clue you in a bit. Hell House is a live theatrical outreach event set up like a typical haunted house. Visitors are taken on a seven-scene journey, each one portraying the consequences of a sinful choice.[17] Drinking and driving, smoking, taking drugs, and abortion are all presented in unblinking and gruesome detail. At the end, spiritual spectators are presented with the option to choose between the glories of heaven or the fires of hell. In honesty, this sappy spectacle should give participants a third option—I want my money back.

While these horror stories make good potential plotlines for *Left Behind*-esque thrillers, dudes like Dawkins cannot conclude on the basis of these spiritual spectacles that "religious education is brainwashing and child abuse."[18] As Tom Gilson, a strategic planner for Campus Crusade for Christ, observes, "If religious training is thought to be child abuse, an obvious scientific hypothesis follows: Children with religious upbringings should show some of the symptoms that are typical of abused children."[19] One cannot find a comprehensive study that proves religious education per se leads to depression, low self-esteem, substance abuse, and other factors present in those children who have been subjected to prolonged actual abuse, albeit of a religious or secular nature.

How many times am I going to have to say that the fringe does not represent the faithful before it starts to sink in here? I dunno about you, but I about lost my lunch when I learned that Fred Phelps pickets the funerals of US servicemen killed in Iraq simply because these fallen heroes were fighting for a country with a pro-homosexual agenda.[20] Phelps, Robertson, and Coulter are three individuals who claim to be Christian. Nothing more. Nothing less. So stop touting them as say-no-more proof that all Christians are kooks. Do you really want me trolling around the offices of, say, *Paranoia* magazine for the scientific equivalent of this tripe?[21] I didn't think so.

While the Christian community runs the gamut when it comes to hot-button issues such as homosexuality, the vast majority of us would never dream of saying, "God hates fags," blaming the 9/11 terrorist attacks on gays and lesbians, or calling 2008 Democratic presidential candidate John Edwards a "faggot."[22] Our application of the Christian faith leads the vast majority of us away from spewing such venom.

I'm not saying we're perfect. Heck, I am sure if you tried, you could find people who have been at the end of one of my angry rants who would say I am anything but Christlike. I could list examples of where I've blown it big-time, but it wouldn't be fair to the people I've wronged for me to air my dirty laundry out in public. Trust me, I am no saint. Far from it. But when I let my anger get the better of me, I apologize to God. Then I try to reach out to the person I offended and let him or her know I blew it.[23]

With that said, I wouldn't call Phelps, Robertson, or Coulter unrepentant in the slightest. No siree. I'm not condemning them (that's God's job, not mine), only pointing out that—like Howard Stern, Rosie O'Donnell, and Don Imus—their public careers depend on their shock-jock abrasiveness. Sure, sometimes they might say "sorry," but it's more of an "oops, you got me" face-saving move. I have yet to see among either trio any attempt to achieve genuine reconciliation with those they have wronged by their words and deeds.

Blaming all Christians for the unrepentant bad behavior of a few sick souls is akin to listing C. S. Lewis, J. R. R. Tolkien, and G. P. Taylor, and then saying that all Christians are British best-selling fantasy authors. Using that logic, why not pick the documentary *Jesus Camp* as evidence that all Christian summer camps train kids to be foot soldiers in God's Army? Let's see, *The Left Behind: Eternal Forces* real-time strategy game could be used to prove all Christians are militant prayer warriors for Christ. Any National Council of Churches USA conference could lead anyone to assume that all Christians are squishy, spineless, spiritual saps.[30] Heck, hit up a Christian music festival and you're liable to conclude that Christians are stoned on granola 'cause golly gee whiz, they're just so durn "Spirit-filled." Log on to select influential emergent church bloggers meetups, and you'll be convinced you can't participate in this discussion if you don't have at least two of the requisite three Ps: PhD, published author, and pastor/church planter (complete with goatee).

If that's the game you want to play, then how about if I turn the tables around here a bit? I could pick out, say, the Marquis de Sade, Woody Allen, and Marilyn Manson. I can use their stories to prove that all atheists are sadists, dirty old men, and really bad rock musicians. Then I can trek over to Comic Con International: San Diego, where I'll find ample proof that atheists worship Stan Lee and like to pretend they're superheroes. Also, I could run through a list of anti-God dictators, who demonstrate the full range of cruelties that atheists can impose on all of humanity when they rise to power. In addition, I could go to open mic night at just about any comedy club in the country and watch enough Bill Maher wannabes bomb that I could conclude that atheists can't do stand-up comedy worth squat.

Trust me, we both can find fringe fanatics to prove the other side is nutso. So let's stop with this stereotypical silliness.

People like Phelps give a lot of spiritual seekers like myself the heebie-jeebies. I, for one, tend to break out in hives, spiritually speaking, whenever Christians start to think they're above the law and forget to follow the teachings of the risen Christ. Just because we don't put our faith into practice much of the time doesn't mean that we've given up on God.

Having said that, when we as Christians hear of atrocities being done under the guise of religion, we need to be a vocal body and denounce anyone who defiles the word of God in such a heinous fashion. I know facing up to a Phelps figure is rough business, which is why we need to rise up together and beat down these bullies. If we stay silent, then we let their actions define the Christian faith that we claim to practice.

Are there real physical dangers to raising our voices in the name of Christ? You betcha. Why do you think so many of us, myself included, choose silence over suffering?

Nora Gallagher, author of *Practicing Resurrection*, reminds us of the sacrifice of faithful followers such as German pastor Dietrich Bonhoeffer, who was hanged in 1945 by the Nazis for his participation in a plot to assassinate Hitler.

> [He] believed that the heart of what it meant to be a Christian was to act on behalf of the marginalized—the helpless, the sick, the poor, the friendless. He distinguished between what he called "cheap grace," that form of lip service I think we can all identify with, and "costly grace," meaning the kind that gets you into trouble.[24]

Here's a modest proposal: Instead of whining 24/7 about church catastrophes, why don't these New Atheists take some time to really get to know people of faith. How about checking out the good that has been done in the name of religion?

You could start by going to Yad Vashem in Israel, as I did in January 2007. Here you'll see that in the garden of remembrance, there are markers commemorating those (including Christians) who helped their fellow brothers and sisters escape the horrors of the Holocaust. Or if you want something a bit closer to home, trek over to The Simple Way in South Philly and watch a group of ordinary radicals transform a neighborhood through simple, yet radical acts of kindness.[25]

During Habitat for Humanity's 2000 Jimmy Carter Work Project in New York City, I watched as then Mayor Rudy Giuliani and former President Jimmy Carter set aside their political differences and worked together to help build twenty-two affordable housing units for New Yorkers in need. After 9/11, the New York City Habitat chapter responded to this massive destruction by bringing together Jewish, Christian, and Muslim groups to help rebuild neighborhoods in Brooklyn and the Bronx that had been ravaged by urban violence. Try picking up a hammer and join in this interfaith effort to rebuild communities instead of hammering on the faithful, and see what happens. When I first set foot on a building site back in 1999, I know I probably caused more harm than good. But if I can learn rudimentary carpentry skills, anyone can.

These are but a few of the many concrete examples of Christians living out the Great Commandment, "'You shall love the LORD your God with all your heart, with all your soul, and with all your mind.' This is the first and great commandment. And the second is like it: 'You shall love your neighbor as yourself.'"[26]

Armchair academics can cuddle up with some Dietrich Bonhoeffer and Martin Luther King, with a bit of Gandhi thrown in as a pacifist pleasure.[27] Heck, history's filled with Christians who've bucked the established religious order and put their faith and lives on the line. But I get the sense here that Harris and his New Atheist buds have no interest in engaging in any semblance of a serious dialogue with people of faith.

Right after the 2004 election, Beliefnet.com ran a piece titled "The Twelve Tribes of American Politics,"[28] which divided the electorate into categories including Heartland Cultural Warriors, Convertible Catholics, Seculars, and Spiritual but not Religious. While I would have broken down the categories even further, this short Web piece does highlight the diversity among Americans when it comes to our faith practices. We may be one body in Christ, but we aren't cookie-cutter Christians baked from the same batch of devotional dough.[29]

MUSHY MODERATES

In the 21st century: all books, including the Koran, should be fair game for flushing down the toilet without fear of violent reprisal.[30]
—Sam Harris

I can think of plenty of books worthy of tossing into the john, but I think I'll leave the Qur'an and the Bible alone, thank you. Harris, though, carries on with his commode chatter by spewing some of his most raucous rants all over religious moderates. Sammy says that when it comes to matters of faith, silence is not golden but slanderous. "The very ideal of religious tolerance—born of the notion that every human being should be free to believe whatever he wants about God—is one of the principal forces driving us toward the abyss."[31] He seems to think that anyone who tries to build bridges among those of different faith backgrounds symbolizes one of those squishy sorts preaching a spongy spirituality.

As someone who has spent way too much time trying to get these spineless saps to speak up, I have to say Harris has a point. Like many in the moderate camp, I despise having extremists force-feed their ideology to me as though I were some goose getting prepped to be some fanatic's foie gras treat. But cowering under the covers when confronted by these New Atheist monsters or fanatical spooks is child's play. And yep, there are times when I've chickened out 'cause I just don't feel like dealing with the bullies. Still, that's no excuse. We all need to grow a backbone and learn to stand on our own two spiritual feet.

One of my favorite smart-alecky Web sites, Society for Mutual Autopsy, strikes a resonant chord against such moderate madness:

> As much as I appreciate the kindness with which moderate-to-liberal Christian theologians and practitioners make room for fundamentalists at the table, I can not [sic] put to bed a gnawing suspicion that doing so mistakes civility for rightness and results in a uniquely postmodern mish-mash of opinions which seem to be willing to sacrifice truth for peaceful coexistence.[32]

Before moderates can speak the truth, they first need to be able to articulate what exactly it is they believe. Yes, everyone wants love and peace in the same way everyone likes puppies . . . and daisies. These tangible things give us a nice sense of the warm fuzzies. But if we can't articulate why we follow Christ, then we're gonna get slammed, and rightfully so.

According to Harris, religious moderates represent nothing more than "people talking about just wanting meaning in their lives, which I argue is a total non sequitur when it comes down to justifying your belief in God."[33] Once again, Harris paints all moderates with the same wussie brush, and in doing so, he does a really sloppy paint job, aka Huckleberry Finn.

Miroslav Volf, director of the Yale Center for Faith & Culture, offers this critique. "Most Christians believe that while the Bible was inspired by God. Do they therefore think that it is made up of a collection of free-floating, megaphone pronouncements out of nowhere by God? Absolutely not."[34] Terry Eagleton laments, "Dawkins fails to comprehend that for mainstream Christianity, reason, argument, and honest doubt have always played an integral role in belief."[35] This does not mean, however, that we check ourselves into the Holistic Hospital for Spinal Removal whenever others do dastardly deeds in the name of God. Christians should all take note of Dennett's apt criticism of moderation run amok. "The moderates in all religions *are being used* by the fanatics, and should not only resent this; they should take whatever steps they can to curtail it in their own tradition"[36]

In our personal quest for piety or perhaps fear that the religious extremists will start firing at us, we have stayed silent too long. Our collective failure to articulate and live out what it means to live as a follower of Christ has allowed the fanatics to redefine what it means to be a true follower of the faith. Christian blogger Andrew Jones reflects on a BBC special that pitted fallen televangelist Ted Haggard against anti-God guru Richard Dawkins. When the topic of miracles arose in relation to Ted's eyewitness accounts of medical healings in Columbia, Jones recounted how Ted failed to recount the supernatural realities he had witnessed. As Jones notes, "A religion with no power will become a haunt for demons and a place for decay to set in. And it will leave the church struggling to find rational answers for realities that are mysterious and supernatural and not easily boxed up in scientific terms." After all, isn't faith a transformative life-changing experience where, as Jones reminds his fellow Christians, "Once I was blind, but now I see"?[37]

Sometimes silence isn't golden. Take 9/11, for instance. After all, this was the event that triggered Harris to write his book *The End of Faith* after he realized the role that religious moderates played in providing cover for fundamentalism.[38] Dawkins reports that after 9/11, "the last vestige of respect for the taboo disappeared as I watched the 'Day of Prayer' in Washington Cathedral."[39] Apparently what many believers consider to be genuine attempts at "interfaith dialogue," where disparate groups, seeing the need, come together to find common ground from which to work together, Dawkins dismisses as goofy gatherings of "mutually incompatible faiths."

Unfortunately, as I reported in *Red and Blue God, Black and Blue Church*, the international religious unity that was on full display as soon as the Twin Towers fell was soon replaced by a quest for Old Testament vengeance, coupled with in-fighting among warring religious groups over who should gain media supremacy and book deals for their "heroic" actions during the 9/11 recovery effort.[40] It pained me to write about that, and it still almost brings tears to my eyes whenever I see people who claim to be religious leaders use 9/11 or any other tragedy as an opportunity to push their personal profiles and line their pocketbooks.

If this was all there was to the story of 9/11, I'd join forces with the New Atheists in thinking September 11 proved religion is a complete fraud. But amid all the efforts to make 9/11 memorable, manageable, and marketable, I still see glimmers of healing and hope. Every time a group of us serves in a Salvation Army canteen at a fire, FDNY or NYPD funeral, disaster drill, or some other event, I feel that we are able to somehow respond to the firefighters and police officers in the spirit of radical hospitality that was started at 9/11.[41] Check out the nonprofit organization Where To Turn if you want to see but one of the many grassroots examples of how some of those impacted by 9/11 have chosen to respond to this horrific tragedy by extending the arm of compassion and acting with humility, not hubris.[42]

THE RAINBOW CONNECTION

By painting the religious community in such monochromatic color and staying fixated on 9/11, Harris does capture the worst abuses of the faith. Unfortunately, his one-dimensional snapshots miss the multihued rainbow of ordinary radicals, who get down and dirty and live out the gospel on a daily basis. Shane

Claiborne, founder of The Simple Way, gets to the heart of the problem with his gentle, yet piercing wit.

> When the church becomes a place of brokerage rather than an organic community, she ceases to be alive. The church becomes a distribution center, a place where the poor go to get stuff and the rich come to dump stuff. Both go away satisfied (the rich feel good, the poor get clothed and fed) but no one is transformed. No radical new community is formed. And Jesus did not set up a program, but modeled a way of living that incarnated the reign of God.[43]

Yes, I agree with the New Atheists that too many churches worship a dead dude instead of celebrate the risen Christ. After all, we're supposed to pass the peace, not the prunes. Whenever we present ourselves as religious relics, then we have no real ammo to respond to Harris's claims on *The Colbert Report* that, "the God that's getting people killed is the God who thinks martyrdom is a legitimate metaphysical principle."[44] On the surface, Harris is right; that depiction of God is indeed deadly. Lord only knows how many geeky men would sacrifice themselves here on earth if they knew that seventy-two comely virgins were waiting for them up there beyond the Pearly Gates. If this is the only view of God that the New Atheists see, no wonder they take us to task for being faith fakers.

But when we start to live out the radical teachings of the risen Christ, just think of what can happen. When asked the question, "What is the significance of the cross and the Crucifixion of Jesus?" Marcus Borg responded, "The Christian life becomes about something else, namely, living within this framework of radical trust in God and relationship to God that makes possible our transformation, and, ideally and ultimately, the transformation of the world."[45]

The spiritual life keeps us aware that our
true house is not the house of fear, in which
the powers of hatred and violence rule, but
the house of love, where God resides.[46]

—Henri Nouwen

The Wrath of
Sam Harris
Takes on the
Compassionate
Christ:
Get Ready to
Rumble!

If I could wave a magic wand and get rid of either rape or
religion, I would not hesitate to get rid of religion.[1]

—Sam Harris

SIXTY-FIVE PERCENT OF THOSE POLLED BY THE PEW
Center believe that religion plays a significant role in most wars
and conflicts in the world.[2] A recent *Newsweek* poll conducted in
March 2007 concluded that the American public is still split over
whether religion has too much (32 percent) or too little (31 percent) influence on American politics. Democrats tend to fall in
the "too much" camp (42 percent of them, as opposed to 29 percent who see too little influence). Republicans take the opposite

view (42 percent too little; 14 percent too much). In the poll, 68 percent of respondents said they believed someone could be moral and an atheist, compared to 26 percent who said it was not possible.[3]

In sifting through all this polling data, I can't find any credible statistics proving that rape causes less harm than religion. Once again, Harris goes for shock over scholarship as he makes yet another headline-grabbing pronouncement that's cleverly designed to raise his public profile and enhance his pocketbook. One can only assume that he has limited compassion at best for those victims of rape who seek spiritual solace as they heal from this horrific tragedy.

As always, New Atheists take any statistics that show the underbelly of religion and then push these numbers to extremes. The role of religion in inciting global violence remains their numero uno reason why religion must be abolished. In their minds, should religion be allowed to continue, civilization as we know it will cease to exist.

Something tells me these guys might want to reread their history books a bit. A trek to any museum will show that from the earliest moment of recorded history, humanity had this need to connect with something beyond this earthly realm. Nigel Spivey, fellow of Emmanuel College at Cambridge University, observes, "Forty thousand years ago humans start to bury each other properly, and they start with these burials to put down flowers, gifts, and other signs of what we take to be some kind of succor or consolation, and possibly a belief in an afterlife."[4]

Also, if this analogy were really true—that religion runs

amok to the point where humanity is wiped off the map—then why are we still here? Let's face it, there have been plenty of times when plagues, crusades, and other catastrophes could have crushed religion as an ancient relic, never to return. Why religion has remained a vital part of so many people's lives throughout the centuries can be debated ad infinitum, but not discarded.

But try telling that to these warmongers of words. Should you choose to confront these dudes, be prepared to meet their wrath. From what I can see, the carnage ain't purty.

For example, radio talk-show host Dennis Prager and Harris engaged in a four-day e-mail exchange of ideas on *Jewcy*, an online ideas-and-culture magazine. As they explored the topic, "Why Are Atheists So Angry?" this debate became more akin to a verbal boxing match than a reasoned exchange of words.[5]

Like Prager, I have no clue how to respond when Harris concludes that because Stalin attended a Christian seminary as a youth, obviously religion must bear some of the responsibility for his atrocities. Prager tried to reason that "Stalin was a passionate atheist who murdered untold numbers of Christian clergy, destroyed virtually every church in Russia, and forced Soviet students to study 'scientific atheism.'"[6] But Harris just seemed to put his fingers in his ears and chant, "nanny nanny boo boo" at the top of his lungs. He not only looks like Ben Stiller, but he sometimes acts like him as well.[7]

While Andrew Sullivan never took off the gloves with Harris, he, too, was unable to make any headway during their debate on Beliefnet.com.[8] If these two manly men can't get Harris to sit still and reason, I doubt I'll have any better luck.

RELIGION VS. GOD

I do understand why some people today just throw up their hands and decide it's easier not to believe. Brian McLaren is right on the money when he laments:

> Atheism, I believe, becomes more popular when religious communities become more corrupt—and especially when their corruption includes violence. This occurred in the decades after the Thirty Years War in European history, and I think we're entering a similar period today. When religion seems to produce violent or arrogant or hypocritical believers, many people decide it is more ethical not to believe."[9]

McLaren continues his on-target assessment.

> When the world's second largest religion seems (to many people) too tolerant of terrorism and sectarian violence, and sometimes even encourages and justifies them, we shouldn't be surprised that many people reject religion. When the world's largest religion seems (to many people) too tolerant of militarism, unjustified war, and consumerism, and sometimes even encourages and justifies them, we should be even less surprised.
>
> When both religions do too little to promote active peacemaking, care for the poor, concern for the environment, and the renewal of communities, when they seem more concerned with "straining out gnats" of religious trivia than "swallowing camels" of massive social injustice, we should only be surprised that more people haven't become atheists.[10]

Clearly many atheists weigh the evidence for and against the existence of God and then conclude God does not exist. But what McLaren references here is the presentation of faulty data by the Christian community that contradicts the teachings of Jesus Christ. How can we expect anyone to buy into this Bible biz if we don't practice what we preach? Too many Christians forget that we are to be the salt of the earth, and hence they're serving up bland versions of the faith instead of the real meal deal.[11] But please let's not give up on God. The cluelessness is with us, not the Almighty. After all, God gave humanity free will from the get-go.[12]

Furthermore, blaming religion for all the world's woes neglects the simple fact that violence and degradation against one's fellow man is not limited to the religious sphere. Ever since Cain slew Abel, humans have had a proven propensity for violence.[13] It's part of our hard wiring. Go to any museum and you'll see plenty of ghastly paraphernalia that's been used throughout the centuries to disfigure, torture, and kill the other. Yes, much of this carnage was done in the name of some state-sanctioned version of religion, but a lot of these affliction apparatuses have no religious connotation whatsoever. How many vile, gross, and disgusting acts would I have to parade around before it becomes obvious that people have done horrific things to one another from the start of recorded history?

DEFINING RELIGION?

We need to be sure we've got our terminology correct. According to the *Merriam-Webster's Online Dictionary*, "religion" can be defined as: "1) the service and worship of God or the super-natural; 2) commitment or devotion to religious faith or obser-vance; 3) *archaic:* scrupulous conformity; or 4) a cause, principle, or system of beliefs held to with ardor and faith."[14]

I'm surmising, based on Webster's definition of religion, that any set of beliefs, secular or religious, could be imposed on others by force. Whether or not God, money, power, or sex (I think I've covered the biggies here) is used as the justi-fication for said beliefs appears to be irrelevant. The end result remains that one group desires to achieve dominion by any means necessary.

Harris defends secular-inspired violence committed by athe-ist ideologies in China and the old Soviet Union by claiming that these regimes operated under a rubric he calls "political reli-gions."[15] Using the term "religion" in this context suggests a rigid ideology used by those in power to control the masses instead of a God-centered form of worship.

Charles Taylor ponders how defining Communism as a reli-gion "means that any set of beliefs which can induce decent people, who would never kill for personal gain, to murder for the cause, is being defined as religion. 'Religion' is being defined as the murderously irrational."[16] "Religion doesn't make people bigots. People are bigots and they use religion to justify their ideology,"[17] adds Reza Aslan, author of *No God but God*, a history of Islam.[18] Bingo.

 I don't know anyone less Jesus-like
than most Christians.[19]
—Bill Maher

David Kuo reported on his blog about his brief appearance on *Real Time with Bill Maher*. He admits he was tapped in via satellite, so he didn't get the full-on audience participation dealie. But he commented that "at some point, in response to a question, I said that yes, Jesus actually does love everyone and that includes Democrats and liberals and homosexuals. The audience just erupted in applause. Here is the simple takeaway—people love Jesus, they just disapprove of his self-appointed PR people who portray him as political and narrow and angry."[20] Even avowed atheist Bill Maher concurs that if we believe in a Jesus who endorses war, antienvironmental policies, and the like, "then you might as well believe bunnies lay painted eggs."[21]

Once again, bingo. Two for two. I like these Catholic Church odds.

So let's start to get the heat off God and His Son and put it back where it belongs—at the foot of those who sync His agenda with their own whims as if the Almighty were their own beloved BlackBerry.[22]

Digging the Dude

I fail to see where Jesus would support bringing to bear the full force of the godhead to justify any violence whatsoever. In fact, if you reread the New Testament (hint, hint), you'll see there are times when even His disciples get pretty ticked off at their leader. Apparently, they were expecting a Messiah who would usher in a violent revolution against the Romans to recapture Jerusalem.[23] They were all rough 'n' ready for some good old-fashioned hiney kickin', but they got this dude on a donkey instead.

In fact, as Steve Chalke, MBE, founder of Oasis Global & Faithworks, points out, "The Pharisees went absolutely berserk because Deuteronomy says [that] the disabled should be kept out of the assembly."[24] Boy, did Jesus give them an earful. Kinda makes me wonder what keeps the Christian community from cutting loose like this whenever those in power misuse and distort the gospel. Guess they're too busy calling Jesus their homeboy to contemplate what moves the Man would make when faced with those in religious power who tried to maintain the status quo.

Chalke reminds us that the current temple system represented "Israel's huge giant apartheid filtration system, where only those with the right DNA and the right moral standing and status in society could get in."[25] This troublemaker broke down every conceivable barrier that stood in the way of making God's grace and love available to all of humanity. This was no simple anger-management issue. According to Chalke, in smashing the moneychangers' tables, "Jesus brings the whole temple system to a grinding halt—if only temporarily, at that stage." This closed caste system so beloved by the Pharisees came tumbling down. And that's what got him killed. Chalke adds, "If Jesus was the kind of goody-goody that he's presented as, then the Jews and Romans wouldn't have crucified him."[26]

While there's much to ridicule about the Pharisees, perhaps we should stop making fun of the speck in their eye and deal with the plank that's blinding us. Just like the religious leaders of Jesus' era, too many contemporary Christians fall into the trap of worshipping religion instead of seeking God. As part of our fallen human nature, we tend to market Jesus Christ™ according to our own personal desires.[27] But God has a way of bursting through and breaking down whatever preconceived selfish notions we may have. In the end, the kingdom of God wins hands down.[28] No contest.

Brian McLaren reflects on Jesus' radical plan to open up God's kingdom to all. "He isn't talking about just going or not going to hell after you die. He's talking about a radical different way of living. He's talking about changing the world and living in a subversive and radical way in this world."[29]

Those who follow Christ often face the same obstacles. Shane Claiborne went to Iraq out of his convictions that the "message [of the cross] is that there is something worth dying for, but there is nothing worth killing for."[30] This whole living out a life of nonviolence is powerful stuff. Sure, it's scary, but it's the only way. Something tells me history will demonstrate how the powerful, positive, and, dare I say, spiritual legacies of Martin Luther King Jr., Gandhi, and Mother Teresa will far outlive the demented souls who mangle and make havoc of the faith.

LOVE THINE ENEMY?

I gotta admit that one side of me feels like smacking some sense into these New Atheists. They really do make me angry. But my faith tells me to turn the other cheek and not repay violence with violence, to model a "better way."

Jesus laid it on the line in the gospel of Matthew: "But I tell you not to resist an evil person. But whoever slaps you on your right cheek, turn the other to him also."[31] Once again, Jesus turns social convention on its head, encouraging His followers to practice what seems like a perverse form of justice. Is this risky?

You betcha.

Dr. Walter Wink, professor emeritus of biblical interpretation at Auburn Theological Seminary, offers this succinct teaching on the symbolism behind Jesus' words:

Most people picture a blow with the right fist. But that would land on the left cheek, and Jesus specifies the right cheek. A left hook wouldn't fit the bill either, since the left hand was used only for unclean tasks, and even to gesture with it brought shame on the one gesturing. Jesus is speaking about striking the right cheek with the back of the right hand. This was not a blow to injure. It was symbolic. It was intended to humiliate, to put an inferior in his or her place. It was given by a master to a slave, a husband to a wife, a parent to a child, or a Roman to a Jew. The message of the powerful to their subjects was clear: You are a nobody, get back down where you belong . . . By turning the other cheek, the person struck puts the striker in an untenable spot. He cannot repeat the backhand, because the other's nose is now in the way. The left cheek makes a fine target, but only persons who are equals fight with fists, and the last thing the master wants is for the slave to assert equality.[32]

I dunno about you, but the idea of making myself totally vulnerable scares the bejesus out of me. But as Henri Nouwen reminds me:

Turning the other cheek means showing our enemies that they can be our enemies only while supposing that we are anxiously clinging to our private property, whatever that is:

our knowledge, our good name, our land, our money, or the many objects we have collected around us. But who will be our robber when everything he wants to steal from us becomes our gift to him? Who can lie to us, when only the truth will serve him well? Who wants to sneak into our back door, when the front door is wide open? Poverty makes a good host.[33]

During the height of the Bosnian War, I asked Miroslav Volf if there isn't a real danger that turning the other cheek could lead to violence and oppression.

Will the exchange of blows lead to peace and justice? I very much doubt that. And if it did, that peace would in fact be violence portraying itself as peace, and that justice would in fact be oppression parading as justice. It is important to underscore that Christians do not turn the other cheek because this is the most effective way to combat violence and oppression. If this were the case, once the effectiveness of this strategy were no longer obtained, they could switch from commitment to nonviolence to engagement in violence.[34]

Now, you know what's coming next. So, what if this turning-the-cheek thingy doesn't work? Can we then kick our enemies where it really hurts? Nope. Don't go there.

Volf adds, 'The best response I know—a response that merits careful pondering—is the one given by the late John Howard Yoder: 'The relationship between the obedience of God's people and the triumph of God's cause is not a relationship of cause and effect, but one of cross and resurrection.'''[35]

Amen, brother. Perhaps if these New Atheist dudes would spend as much time pondering Wink's and Volf's words of wisdom as they do trash-talking the faithful, we could have a reasoned and sane discussion. But that's a long shot. It'll take a miracle for that to happen, and that's God's job, not mine. Still it's something worth praying for, that's for sure.

Tutu Talks

In the meantime, I would encourage every atheist who blames religion for all the world's woes to pick up a copy of Archbishop Desmond Tutu's book, *No Future Without Forgiveness*. Throughout this book, you can see the invisible hand of God at work as Tutu relays the story of how the Truth and Reconciliation Commission (TRC) came together to unite the battered nation of South Africa. In assessing the work of the TRC, Tutu offers this sage commentary, "It was God's intention to bring all things in heaven and on earth to a unity in Christ, and each of us participates in this grand movement."[36]

Despite some admitted human flaws present within the structure of the TRC, this vehicle created a safe and sacred space where victims and perpetrators could come together to tell their respective stories. As N. T. Wright astutely observes:

> The fact of white security forces and black guerrillas both confessing in public to their violent and horrific crimes is itself an awesome phenomenon. And with those confessions, the families of the tortured and murdered have been able for the first time to begin the process of true grieving, and

thereby to at least contemplate the possibility of being able to forgive."[37]

He adds, "I have no hesitation in saying that the fact that such a body is even existing, let alone doing the work it has done, is the most extraordinary sign of the power of the Christian gospel in my lifetime.[38]

More recently, the agreement between the factions involved in the Northern Ireland peace process has shown how violent conflict between religio-ethnic groups can be resolved through both peaceful means and the involvement of religious peacemakers. Belfast-based writer and acvtivist Dr. Gareth Higgins says, "The conflict in N. I. is not exclusively religious, but it has a religious component. It was necessary, therefore, that religion be employed as part of the process of transforming the conflict. Religious leaders, motivated by their commitment to Christian nonviolence played a significant role in contributing to the conditions for peace, through dialogue, education, and other forms of courageous witness. It is not accurate to say that without religion, there would have been no conflict; but without religious peacemakers, there may well not have been peace."[39]

These two stories are two small but significant examples of godly faith in action, a power that no earthly violence can ever wipe off the map completely. Thanks be to God, 'cause Lord knows these man-made mountains of violence and oppression don't seem to get moved without some kind of divine intervention.

WHY HAVE YOU FORSAKEN ME?

> If he existed and chose to reveal it,
> God himself could clinch the argument,
> noisily and unequivocally, in his favor.[1]
>
> —RICHARD DAWKINS

> If God is omniscient and omnipotent, you can't
> help wondering why she doesn't pull out a
> thunderbolt and strike down Richard Dawkins.[2]
>
> —NICHOLAS D. KRISTOF, THE *NEW YORK TIMES*

OK. I ADMIT KRISTOF TOOK A CHEAP SHOT—
though you gotta admit one of those Zeus-like thunderbolts
would be a convenient way for God to end this debate once and
for all.

Not to worry, I am not about to launch an "Annihilate All
Atheists" campaign. We've already established that I'm a real
wuss when it comes to actual war. Remember, I'm the one who
wants us to play in our respective sandboxes. They're the ones
who want to take away my bucket and shovel and even destroy
my sandcastle.

I do have this urge, though, to kick some sand in the face of whoever designed this godforsaken Web site titled Why Won't God Heal Amputees?[3] This slimy site oozes snark, but without the redemptive bite that makes for quality satire. Throughout the Web pages, the authors keep asking ad nauseum why God never helps poor amputees. After all, the Almighty answers prayers for miraculous cures for those suffering from cancer, rabies, and other terminal ailments. So why not throw these guys a bone and actually grow a new limb for them? What gives here?

To this query of divinity, Nicolas Kristof responds:

> God may not help amputees sprout new limbs, but churches do galvanize their members to support soup kitchens, home- less shelters, and clinics that otherwise would not exist. Religious constituencies have pushed for more action on AIDS, malaria, sex trafficking, and Darfur's genocide, and believers often give large proportions of their incomes to charities that are a lifeline to the neediest.[4]

As a religious satirist, I am well aware of the healing hooey done by Benny Hinn & Company.[5] But I've also witnessed my share of miracles that defy any credible description.

Yes, I can hear the New Atheists' all-too-common lament: How come you religious folk are enabling your Holy Father? Why should humanity be responsible for cleaning up your God's garbage? I mean, you wouldn't have to set up any clinics whatso- ever if your God didn't create these diseases in the first place, right?

According to their highly unscientific postmortem on God, events such as September 11 and Hurricane Katrina provide irrefutable proof that God does not exist. After all, this is the Almighty we're talking about, not some surly teenager who blames the family dog every time he messes up. Surely an omnipresent, omnipotent, and supposedly *good* transcendent being can pick up after himself.

This simplistic assertion assumes that God's Old Testament modus operandi—showing up in rolling thunderclouds or appearing as a column of fire and smoke—can be applied unilaterally without taking into account the other ways God is revealed both in the Bible and throughout the human story. You have the God who kicks hiney, a God who brings peace, a God who demands you join His private Jewish-only country club, a God who welcomes all into His Kingdom, a God who watches over His people, and a God who lets bad things happen to good people.

What's amazing is not that so many varieties exist, but that the biblical authors embraced these inconsistencies. They were not troubled by our modern need to make everything all neat and tidy, so by the end of the sixty-minute Sunday service, God has been signed, sealed, and delivered. Salvation's waiting for you at the altar call. Then next Sunday, it's read, rinse, and repeat. And the spin cycle continues. If that's all I knew about God, I'd probably be an atheist too. Sounds dreadful. Rather, these ancient authors embraced the inherent messiness of God.

In AD 325 the First Council of Nicea came up with a draft copy of what eventually became the Nicene Creed, the oldest and most ecumenically accepted Christian statement of faith. The Nicene Creed acknowledges the multifaceted nature of God: "We believe in one God the Father Almighty, Maker of heaven and earth, of all that is seen and unseen." These New

Atheists respond with a fat raspberry. In their worldview, anything they cannot experience with their five senses must be bogus. Yes, there is great variety among the different depictions of God in the Old and New Testaments. But the presence of multiple meanings for God doesn't deliver believers over to spiritual schizophrenia. Postmodern philosopher Peter Rollins aptly observes, "Such fissures help to prevent us from forming an idolatrous image of God."[7] As we seek to understand God, we are bound by the limits of our own humanity. We simply cannot take in the full picture of who God is. But we can catch fleeting glimpses of God through theses biblical tensions and contractions. Rollins reflects, "Revelation embraces concealment . . . this means our various interpretations of revelation will always be provisional, fragile and fragmentary—that we speak always with wounded words about a wounded Christ."[8] Our human and finite brains lack the necessary vocabulary needed to fully articulate our understanding when we experience even these minute and fleeting fragments of the divine. We're literally at a loss for words.

Contemporary Christian confusion often abounds in our need to create literal sense from ancient biblical words. Today's New Atheists and strict biblical literalists alike take the Bible as a factual textbook. By contrast, Mediterranean philosophers and politicians (as well as many people and cultures in eras before and since) communicated their message in poetry and parable, living and breathing beyond the strictures of a rigid scientism. So when Jesus spoke in riddle and story, his hearers weren't content to rest on the literal surface of His words, but they sought to further discern the wisdom inherent in the deep meaning behind His stories.

As New Testament scholar Raymond E. Brown notes, "Because

they are polyvalent, the particular point of parables takes on coloration from the context in which they are uttered or placed."[9] Hence, while representative symbols such as a vineyard, servants, and wedding would have been well-known and understood within their proper sociopolitical context by Jesus' audiences, such phrases can easily be misinterpreted if we view these stories from a twenty-first-century cultural lens.

Furthermore, these seemingly simple stories did not originate with Christ but stemmed from the Wisdom tradition. By employing the rhetorical device of the parable, Jesus used common occurrences to cast light on the divine. Rollins notes how "a parable speaks to 'those with ears to hear'—it is given to us but its meaning is not something that can be reduced to some clear, singular scientific formula, rather there are a multitude of commentaries bringing out different insights."[10]

In *Reluctant Prophets and Clueless Disciples*, Robert Darden reminds his fellow Christians of the personal quality of these parables.[11]

> We self-identify with certain figures in each of the parables. For instance, we unconsciously align ourselves with the Older Brother in the story of the Prodigal Son, or workers who worked all day in the Parable of the Vineyard . . . and we get it *wrong* 100 percent of the time. We're *all* of the people in *all* of the parables. They're not about other people, they're about us. Remember the Pharisee who prays on a street corner and the humble man who won't look at heaven when he whispers a desperate prayer? *We're* the Pharisee! The Samaritan in the Good Samaritan—*we're* the religious types who stepped around the guy who was bleeding on the ground.[12]

Even today, we are presented with parables that can help us understand God's ongoing interactions with His creation. When I interviewed Fr. James Martin, SJ, about his experience serving as a chaplain at Ground Zero after September 11, he explained how the World Trade Center rescue workers were in themselves a modern-day parable that expressed how God will never totally abandon His creation:

> Like any parable, it's a very simple story drawn from real life that, as the Scripture scholars say, teases the mind into active thought. In the parables in the Gospels you have questions like "What is God like?" Jesus uses a number of metaphors such as a mustard seed, a pearl, and a banquet. I would say, "What is God like? God is like the firefighter who goes into the burning building to rescue people." That's a real parable. I think that story of the firefighters and the rescue workers rushing into those burning buildings and giving up their lives affected people because those stories spoke to them in a very deep and spiritual level. But I think God in the midst of this suffering was offering us this very profound parable, this very profound sign of the way He is and the way that God's love is.[13]

Where Is God?

I fully understand why New Atheists like Sam Harris believe an event such as 9/11 proves there is no God. When we're in the midst of our own personal hell, we can't see God's love in action. Nothing makes any sense.

After my parents died, I recall shrieking my teenaged version of Jesus' languishing lament on the cross when He cried out with a loud voice, "My God, My God, why have You forsaken me?"[14] I bawled beyond my bones; the very matter of my marrow became soaked with the stench of sorrow. Stanley Hauerwas, professor of theological ethics at Duke Divinity School and noted author, reflects how Jesus' dying cry "shows that Christ does experience the darkness of being completely alienated from the Father."[15]

So, yes, like the New Atheists, I ranted and swore against the Lord God Almighty like crazy. You name just about any combo of swear words that one can utter taking God's and Jesus' names in vain and I'll betcha I said 'em. I had way too many questions that were simply unanswerable: Why would a loving God allow a toxic substance like alcohol to kill a priest, of all people? Why did God let my mom get sucked into a similar vortex of alcohol and drugs until all the life was sucked out of her and she died?

What did I do to deserve such punishment? As a budding writer, I was already dealing with more than my share of preteen angst and personal weirdness.[16] I realized by the time I was twelve, that I lacked "it," that magic elixir that sent prepubescent boys into hysteria. Now, the quirky and interesting guys were always interested in me, you know, the science-fair geek with the pockmarked skin and the pocket protector, who by now is either a multimillionaire technonerd or another Unabomber type in training; the art student, who wore black long before the color was "cool" and was the only kid in school sporting an earring and a goatee; as well as the other loners in the library.[17] So I already had ample material to fill the pages of any tormented teen diary.

I was suffering enough, thank you. So why did God have to add "orphan" into this deadly cocktail?

Fellow Southern writer—and one of my idols—Flannery O'Connor got it right when she said, "The truth does not change according to our ability to stomach it."[18] Children of alcoholics tend to lose their parents in increments. It's not like a car crash, where—boom—they were here one minute, and now they're gone. Forever. Just like that. And it's not like having a parent with a sympathetic terminal illness, and people come over to your house with homemade casseroles and coffee cake, trying to support you during this "difficult time."

Over time my parents slowly started to lose little pieces of themselves. As they got worse, the shame of my family's demise drove my extended family and all their friends to seek higher ground, leaving us black sheep to forage for ourselves.[19] Bit by bit they started to go. I don't know at what point my parents' souls actually left their bodies, after which, I pray, they were welcomed into God's loving arms. But it was pretty durn clear that by the time we buried them, there was nothing left.

Don't tell me about Adam and Eve, the fall and all that jazz. At that point, I was ready to tell anyone who threw the Bible in my face exactly where they could put the book of Genesis. And if they weren't too careful, I might shove the Pentateuch—or maybe even the entire Old Testament—at 'em too.

Intellectually, I got the concept of free will and how our actions have consequences. But couldn't God have made an exception and given my dad the will to kick his addiction? Why did God seem to be taking a dirt nap as I buried my father and mother within an eleven-month period? This isn't how a sixteen-year-old's life is supposed to go. And if my dad had to die, why did he have to do it on my birthday? Happy Birthday, Sweet Sixteen. Not.

> Wouldn't it be lovely to believe in an imaginary friend who listens to your thoughts, listens to your prayers, comforts you, consoles you, gives you life after death, can give you advice? Of course it's satisfying, if you can believe it. But who wants to believe a lie?[20]
> —Richard Dawkins

I know Dawkins thinks I'm just giving a weepy, wimpy, emotionally laden response to his seemingly flip questions, where I'll win the argument by pulling out the sympathy card. No, this isn't some sappy salvation story that some cheesy Christian ministry can plaster on a tasteless tract and market it to their fellow Jesus jumpers. Trust me. I don't operate like that.

Look, I truly get where he's coming from. Believe me, if my pain were all there was to the story, I would join the New Atheists in decrying those who believe in an imaginary buddy. But my story didn't end in death, but with a new life.

Right before my father's funeral, the priest took the Garrison kids aside. "Even though your father couldn't help himself, he was there for countless others who were lost," he whispered to us, using that voice of professional compassion that's designed to soothe without getting too involved. "I've been getting calls for hours from people saying how much the Reverend Dr. Karl Claudius Garrison Jr. changed their lives," he added.

At the funeral, the priest commanded us to love each other regardless of the personal cost. "Even though love brings pain, it's that one-on-one connection that makes us human and separates us from the other animals. So, as long as we're human, that means we have an obligation to keep on living and loving, loving and dying."[21]

When I was sitting there drenched in death, his words didn't seem to be providing one lick of spiritual solace. His whole spiel sounded like one of those stock sermons that priests deliver when they don't know the person. They're torn between their professional obligation to act "pastoral" and their innate desire to avoid the dysfunctional family in front of them.

Still, somehow those words stuck to me. For reasons I cannot explain, my teenage blues never morphed into clinical depression or worse. I survived the loss of a close friend who committed suicide during my senior year of college, and I lost all but one of my grandparents by the time I turned twenty-five. Yet, the words by some priest I only met once and didn't care for one whit (mild understatement) said something that enabled me to hang on to life like some demented, rabid pit bull. In hindsight, I can see the hand of God working though this unknown priest and a few other kind souls. Their words entered into me like tiny specks of sunlight, illuminating what otherwise was a dark, cavernous pit that stank to high heaven.

I still don't fully comprehend the connection between my parents' death and my subsequent encounters with God. After all, my late father was a civil rights activist in the Carolinas back in the late fifties, and then a sociology professor/progressive priest combo during the turbulent sixties, before devolving and dying during the seventies Me Generation. Had he remained sober, my dad could have had quite the illustrious collegiate Christian career. I could have had stimulating social justice spiritual encounters, hung out with the tragically-hip-yet-holier-than-thou set, and done all that Jesus jazz without losing my parents. Add to it my Southern grandparents' social connections, and after I made my debut, I would have emerged as the perfect limousine liberal, socially responsible but with a conservative's pocketbook to keep me from having to get down and dirty.[22]

But, given I'm a broke religious satirist, who finally quit the Junior League in disgust, that obviously isn't how the story played out. To say that God had different plans for me would be the understatement of the year.

> As we gradually come to befriend our own
> reality, to look with compassion at our
> own sorrows and joys, and as we are able to
> discover the unique potential of our way of
> being in the world, we can move beyond
> our protest, put the cup of our life to our lips,
> and drink it, slowly, carefully, but fully.[23]
> —Henri Nouwen

Reading Henri Nouwen's *The Wounded Healer* started a lifelong journey of learning how to take my childhood hurts and not only be healed through Christ, but use myself as an example to help heal others.[24] Thanks to the works of ancient and contemporary saints such as St. John of the Cross, St. Julian of Norwich, and Gerald May,[25] I've received a miraculous gift of grace. Through their personal struggles, these spiritual guides gave me hope and taught me it's OK to question what's up with God. After all, the Almighty can handle it. He is Lord of all, you know.

> If there were a God, I think it very unlikely that He would have such an uneasy vanity as to be offended by those who doubt His existence.[26]
> —Bertrand Russell

For reasons I'll never understand, these New Atheists can't tolerate living in a world of "unknowing." Their universe is a giant adding machine, where you stamp "forbidden" on those things that just don't add up. I'm just not wired that way. Now, I'm not saying I'm this content bodhisattva. No way, no how. But I'm learning to live in the questions without completely freaking out, and for me that's a good start in the right direction.

When I asked Fr. Martin where was God on September 11, he replied, "I prefer to look at where was God after those things happened. God was very much with the rescue workers. I'm sure God was there in a mysterious way. It's very hard for us as human beings to see where He was at the moment that the planes hit."[27] I confess, I still don't get where God is at the moment of a tragedy. But I do know I am not alone.

Stanley Hauerwas reminds Christians that when people say, "'The world changed on Sept. 11, 2001,' we have to say 'No, the world changed on 33 AD.' The question is how to narrate what happened on September 11 in light of what happened in 33 AD."[28]

Those days when I can actually get still enough to meditate

on the power of the cross and the resurrection, I'm humbled at how I can still stand here as living, breathing proof that you can go to hell and come back reborn and renewed. Ask me to literally explain what happened to me and I can't. God supernaturally altered every aspect of my being. He listened to all of my rants and began a healing process in my soul that will continue for the rest of my life. I know I've been transformed, though I confess there are days when my faults get the better of me and something besides Christ shines through instead.

As I travel along this admittedly crooked spiritual path, I've met other similar souls. Collectively we stand, albeit a bit wobbly, as living proof to the power of God's redemptive and transformative love. Now that we've been to hell and back, we're able to help others out of the pit and into the light. If the New Atheists are too blind to see this, then heaven help them. It's out of our hands.

HOLY HEALING?

Speaking of being clueless, just because you *can* say something doesn't mean it's a good idea. There is this thing called compassion that should take precedence in the midst of a disaster. During the 9/11 recovery effort, I took heat from some radical PC Christians (you know, the ones who protest and party courtesy of their trust funds). They weren't too happy about the fact that I was soliciting donations of American flags and cigarettes. Even though I'm a staunch advocate for the separation of church and state and deplore smoking 'cause I lost a chain-smoking, cussin' Yankee grandma to lung cancer, I sought out these items because they provided comfort to those in crisis. Regardless of how I felt about handing out such contraband, I did it. Sometimes one's ideals should take a backseat, even if only for a brief moment.

When discussing the aftermath of Katrina, Harris blurted out, "Only the atheist has the courage to admit the obvious: These poor people died talking to an imaginary friend."[29] Now, I tell you, was that really necessary? Uh, *courage* isn't exactly the word that comes to mind when I ponder Harris's bereavement techniques.

Admittedly, the religious can also act ridiculous when tragedy hits. While the religious community and not FEMA got Brownie points for responding to the immediate needs of those impacted by Katrina, there was plenty of spiritual silliness going around. Stephen O'Leary, a professor at the Annenberg School for Communication at the University of Southern California and an expert on the media and apocalypticism, observed, "God's got a two-fer here. Both sides are eager to see America punished for her sins; on one side it's sexual immorality and porn and Hollywood, and on the other side it's conspicuous consumption and Hummers."[30]

Evangelist Tony Campolo reminisces about a time when he was appearing on the 700 Club on the same show when Pat Robertson claimed that because of his prayers, God turned the hurricane away from Virginia Beach and the TV station was spared. "What upsets me about stories like that is what they suggest about those who *do* experience tragedies. The implication is that had the victims of Katrina been as spiritual as Pat Robertson, they would have been delivered from the wrath of the storm."[31]

How Christ's overpowering love can transcend such holy

hooey remains for me an ultimate mystery, as well as a continuing source of employment. So far, I have never been at a loss to find faithless fodder. But when I feel like throwing in the towel, I can count on Shane Claiborne to give me a spiritual shoulder to cry on. This Southern soul mate reminds me, "Our discontent with the church is the very reason that we engage rather than pull out. Within the brokenness of the church is our own brokenness."[32]

The Christ-lived life trumps any New Thought–themed schlock that teaches gullible souls to *Forgive for Good* because *Self Matters* as you give yourself *The Gift of Change*.[33] Let the Brights explore the outer frontiers of their collective consciousnesses and engage in meaningless meaning-making exercises and gooey group gobbledygook if it makes them feel good. Simply put, this secular self-exploration misses the transformation and message of God. In the end, participants of such nefarious nonsense end up where they started—isolated and alone. But when broken believers come together to break bread, through the body and blood of Christ, we become redeemed and whole.[34]

Now, I'm not against solitude. As a writer, I spend prolonged periods by myself. Frankly, I think I'm pretty good company. As I'm starting to learn, though, too much solitary silence isn't good for the soul. That's why I find myself hitting the blogosphere, shooting off e-mails, or even making phone calls right before a serious deadline, 'cause I know I gotta connect with my other spiritual buds around the world or else I'll die inside. (And, yeah, sometimes distractions are needed to clear the mind so I can refocus.)

As Jesus told his disciples, "for where two or three are gathered together in My name, I am in the midst of them."[35] When we choose to allow the love of God to shine through the broken bits and pieces of our shattered lives, then we can truly be the body of Christ. By living within this global community of believers, I've learned that despite whatever may happen in this world, God has not forsaken us. Thanks be to God.

ONE NATION UNDER GOD?

Whether they (referring to the founding fathers)
were atheists, agnostics, deists, or Christians,
they would have recoiled in horror from the
theocrats of the early 21st-century Washington.[1]

—RICHARD DAWKINS

HERE WE GO AGAIN, ARCHAIC ARGUMENTS
rehashed. Political junkies already came pretty durn close to
OD'ing on the sea of books, documentaries, articles, and other
media that flooded the market soon after *God's Politics* hit the *New
York Times* best seller list.[2] Even though I contributed to this del-
uge, I have moved beyond just blasting the Beltway as I seek to
dismantle those religious idols that prevent the Christian community from living out our faith in a post-9/11 world. Looks like
Harris & Co. prefer to remain Johnny One Note, harping on bad
Christian behavior ad infinitum. Methinks these men doth
protest too much. Boring.

Can anyone tell me what the significant difference is between
promoting an aggressive "anti-God" agenda versus a hard-line

"pro-family" campaign? I didn't think so. Both factions set their sights on the lowest common denominator in order to get their point across and score political points. And they scare small children.

These guys rant about the separation of church and state as though they invented the concept. Well, uh, they didn't. I hate to be the bearer of bad news, but this concept predates the Constitution. Go back and read the writings of my ancestor Roger Williams, and you will see how his concept of "soul liberty" was in the works way before Thomas Jefferson penned this whole separation-of-church-and-state jazz.[3] If these New Atheists feel they're being persecuted, well, welcome to the club. My poor ol' ancestor got the boot out of godly Massachusetts by my "pure" Puritan relatives, thus setting up a dysfunctional family dynamic that repeats itself whenever someone in my family gets too uppity.[4] To make matters worse, depending on which side of the family you ask, Dad married a damn Yankee or Mom got hitched to this Southern hick. But instead of licking my war wounds like these dudes seem to be doing, I'd rather move forward than relive the past.

Tony Campolo offers a sweet and succinct analysis of the separation-of-church-and-state debate that puts a lot of these current religion-and-politics problems into proper perspective.

> While it is certainly true that the culture of America was highly influenced by Christianity during the Revolutionary and early national periods, the founders of our nation made it a basic principle that neither Christianity nor any other religion would ever be designated as the official religion of our

country. Christian values provided a basis for the high human-
istic values that are inherent in our national character, but it is
wrong to call America a Christian nation. It can easily be
argued that our concept of democracy was derived as much
from the philosophies of the Enlightenment as from the Bible.
In fact, historians tell us that less than 15 percent of those living here in 1776 were members of any church.[5]

Those who keep praying that America returns to her
"Christian roots" would be wise to listen to John D. Caputo's
counsel: "They should be careful about what they pray for lest
their prayers be answered."[6] Somehow, I doubt these contemporary, all-American red, white, and blue Christians could sit
down to high tea with refined eighteenth-century Enlightenment thinkers without having the whole soiree turn into a
Bible brawl.

If these New Atheists could stop their ranting for just a
sec, they'd see that many Christians also recoil in disgust whenever the terms "God" and "America" are used interchangeably.
Yes, there are some Christian leaders who wish to replace the
Religious Right with their own equally vociferous version of
the progressive Left. But a closer examination of this religious-
political debate reveals a much more nuanced picture than the
black-and-white depiction of their faith-and-politics fracas that's
presented by Harris and his New Atheist buds.

On March 12, 2007, I conducted a Google search for "God"
and "politics" and came up with 65,800,000 hits.[7] These Web
sites reveal a plethora of opinions voiced by believers repre-
senting a wide spectrum of the faithful. While we clearly do not

speak with one voice, there is intense interest in examining the interrelationship between church and state.

If the New Atheists weren't so insistent on putting down all Christians, they might find more company in their rallying cry for a strict separation of church and state. But most of us don't want to play in their sandbox for fear they'll throw sand in our faces, or worse. This is a crying shame, because this is one issue where we could really band together and do some good. First we've got to turn down the volume so we can dialogue. The ringing in my ears is starting to drive me nutso!

BAD BUSH BEHAVIOR

 The President of the United States has claimed, on more than one occasion, to be in dialogue with God. If he said that he was talking to God through his hairdryer, this would precipitate a national emergency. I fail to see how the addition of a hairdryer makes the claim more ridiculous or offensive.[8]
—Sam Harris

Harris's hairdryer hooey proves that this best-selling New Atheist writer must have way, way too much free time on his hands. Let's face it, everyone knows Dubya channels Cheney, and Dick hasn't been near a hairdryer in years. 'Sides, if memory serves me correctly, wasn't Bill Clinton the one with the Hollywood-style hair? I wouldn't exactly call Bush stylin'.

Then again, I wouldn't expect these guys to be up-to-date. The anti-God gurus still quote Bush calling Jesus Christ his favorite philosopher.[9] That was so 1999. Come on, get with the twenty-first century.

If they want to rehash old-school political comedy, Dubya's JC bit pales in comparison to Nancy's penchant for astrology, Hillary Clinton's need to channel Eleanor Roosevelt with the assistance of guru Jean Houston, and her hubby Bubba's rewriting of the Ten Commandments so he can keep on being a horndog.[10] Politicians make great fodder for religious satire. Just watch them open up their mouths and the satire just writes itself. Trust me on this one.

By now, I would hope that any sane person realizes that whenever a politician evokes the name of God, it is possible that he or she is simply pandering to a particular voting constituency. *God, Jesus, pro-life, pro-choice, social justice,* and the like are all terms that spin doctors utilize to deftly craft a voter-friendly candidate. Haven't we all been manipulated enough by value-laden language from both sides of the political aisle that we've wised up to these kinda smarmy spiritual moves?

As much as these guys whine about the need to get rid of religion, they tend to wuss out when it comes to enlisting some of their fellow atheists as foot soldiers in the annual war against Christmas. For example, Dennett holds an annual Christmas sing-along, complete with hymns and carols that are not only harmonically lush but explicitly pious.[11] Harris confesses he has a Christmas tree.[12] Even the crusty old Grinch aka Richard Dawkins admits that around the holiday season, this post-Christian atheist, will "unhesitatingly wish everyone a Merry Christmas."[13] Looks like these hardcore atheists have a soft side after all.

THE POLITICS OF FAITH

> Yet if the president of the US started talking about how Saturn was coming into the wrong quadrant and is therefore not a good time to launch a war, one would hope that the whole White House press corps would descend on him with a straitjacket. This would be terrifying—to hear somebody with so much power basing any part of his decision-making process on something as disreputable as astrology. Yet we don't have the same response when he's clearly basing some part of his deliberation on faith.[14]
>
> —Sam Harris

Granted, much of the mainstream media appears to be taking a working vacation. I quit watching White House Press briefings 'cause I don't like throwing things at television sets or my laptop. But please don't imply that we're all turning a blind eye, because we ain't. A host of Christians have been asking WWJD in relation to what's going on inside the Beltway for some time now. It's been more than thirty years since Sojourners moved to Washington DC; Ron Sider wrote his seminal book *Rich Christians in an Age of Hunger*; and the *Wittenburg Door* debuted.[15]

It's not the faithful's fault if we can't get a decent answer. Heck, I'll bet if Jesus came back today and started to roam the halls of the White House or Congress, the powers that be in DC would show Him the door. If He came with His band of disciples, fuggetaboutit. They'd all be arrested lickety-split. His campaign manager looks like one of those crazy homeless guys I see preaching at Times Square, and His female "companion" has an allegedly checkered past that would make Monica Lewinsky blush. He hangs out with tax collectors, drunkards, and a host of other unsavory characters.[16] These aren't the sort you see hanging around Capitol Hill's hallowed watering holes.

I know this isn't the depiction of Jesus most folks get when they step into a church on most Sundays. Like former President Clinton, "I feel your pain."[17] My quest to find a Christian community that at least tries to mirror the gospel has been akin to a Monty Pythonesque search for the Holy Grail. Too many clergy prance around like they're the Minister of Silly Walks[18] instead of trying to be a representative of Christ. Please know that some of us choose not to buy into this whole commercialized Corporate Christ™ dealie.[19] Instead, we seek to follow this trouble-making, rule-breaking, radical love-making Jesus.[20]

Practicing the Politics of Faith

Whenever Christians try to wrap Jesus in the American flag and salute Him with a twenty-one-gun salute, the New Atheists should call us on the carpet for being hypocrites. Mike Yaconelli reflects, "The impotence of today's church, the weakness of Christ's followers, and the irrelevance of most parachurch organizations is directly related to the lack of being in the presence of an awesome, holy God, who continually demands allegiance only to Him—not to our organizations, to our churches or our theology."[21]

Bono echoed this bipartisan spirit when he spoke at the 2006 Presidential Prayer Breakfast. "I keep coming back to Washington because this is a town that is proving it can come together on behalf of what the Scriptures call the least of these. This is not a Republican idea. It is not a Democratic idea. It is not even, with all due respect, an American idea. Nor it is unique to any one faith."[22] Here Bono echoes the best we can be as the body of Christ.

And, yes, such Christian communities can exist. In her book *Christianity for the Rest of Us*,[23] Diana Butler Bass talks about purple churches. Now, she doesn't mean wishy-washy places where everything is blended into a nice Barney-colored hue and we all sing happy-happy-joy-joy songs until we're sick to our stomachs. Barf. Rather, she proclaims, "Early Christians borrowed purple, the color of Roman imperial power, and inverted its political symbolism to stand for their God and God's reign. Christian purple—the color of repentance and humility—represents the kingdom birthed in the martyred church, unified around a crucified savior, and formed by the spiritual authority of being baptized in a community of forgiveness."[24]

As I've stated before and I'll say again, when we as Christians become a political pawn of either party, we lose our ability to be a prophetic witness to the gospel of the risen Christ. If we put partisan politics above seeking the kingdom of God, then we give these New Atheists the tools they need to slam us to smithereens. Frankly, that's the kind of false faith that needs to be dismantled so that the true light of Christ can shine through.

It is in our lives and not from our words
that our religions must be read.[25]
—Thomas Jefferson

I HAVE A DREAM

A medieval cathedral consumed hundreds of
man-centuries in its building. Sacred music
and devotional paintings largely monopolized
medieval and Renaissance talent.[1]

—RICHARD DAWKINS

GRANTED, I'LL CONCEDE THAT MUCH OF WHAT
passes for Christian music is indeed ungodly. Sorry, Carmen—the
Christian singer, not the Bizet opera—Christian cheese just doesn't
cut it for me. If I had my druthers, modern megachurch mega-
plexes would be converted into affordable housing, where at least
their ugliness could do some practical good. I think I'll refrain
from commenting on much of what passes for Christian art.

But, please. How can anyone set foot into the cathedrals of,
say, Notre Dame or Canterbury and not fall to their knees in awe
and wonderment? To dismiss such works of beauty on the grounds
that one's time could have been better spent on nonreligious pur-
suits sounds pretty medieval to me. Does Dawkins really think
Michelangelo and Leonardo Da Vinci wasted their time? Get real.

These sacred works of art would not have stood the test of time if they were simply ways to whittle away the time. Jeez.

Yes, the Catholic Church played patron to these artists, but so what? If you took out all the commissioned art from any major museum, you'd probably end up with a small collection of indigenous art that might be intriguing, but that's about it. (Not all patronizing is bad, right, boys? After all, don't these New Atheists take full advantage of those generous sponsors that underwrite scientific conferences, endowed university chairs, and the like?)[2] Along those lines, reminding Dawkins about how the medieval monks and Islamic scholars kept the Greek philosophical writings from falling into oblivion would be shooting in the dark.

Whenever anyone tries, though, to bring up the positive benefits of religion, the discussion turns back to the number of people banished, maimed, and even killed as a result of their devotion to their gods. Yes, that is true and in some cases tragic. As expected, the New Atheists just want to focus on the "religious" component of the equation here. Somehow in their callous computations of all the religious horrors throughout history, they forget to add in all the hospitals and charities established by religious organizations that provided hope and healing since the Middle Ages.[3]

FAITH NO MORE?

Here's a real puzzlement to hard-core Darwinians. If religion were a truly useless and destructive mechanism with no redemptive quantities whatsoever, then wouldn't faith be extinct by now? At the very least, I expect religion would be akin to an appendix or tonsils. Maybe at one point there was a practical use for an appendix, but by now it's obsolete, though it can prove to be fatal should it become infected. So, if you apply the survival-of-the-fittest motto across the board, then what does it say to us, that religion is still standing? Let's face it. Faith hasn't gone the way of the dodo. Far from it. Like it or not, people continue to perform seemingly heroic acts for their religious beliefs.

Now, clearly this concept of self-sacrifice for the common good cannot be confined to the religious sphere. Throughout history, humanity has similarly sacrificed itself for secular political causes, self-preservation, love of their families, and the like. From the start of recorded time, one can find evidence of humanity's innate need to look beyond self-interest and to care for others. How come?

> Sam Harris: How do you account for my
> altruism?
> Rick Warren: You have common grace. Even
> in people who don't believe in God, there
> is a spark God has put in you that says,
> "There's got to be more to life than just
> make money and die." I think that that
> spark does not come from evolution.[4]

As expected, Dawkins presents a different Purpose-Driven take on Warren's outlook: "Altruism probably has origins like those of lust."[5] Note Dawkins' use of the word "probably." Even he appears to admit that we cannot pinpoint with scientific accuracy why humanity chooses to do good, even when doing so goes against our own self-interests. But if our altruistic genes were simply driven by some primal neanderthal-like pull, then why wouldn't altruism dissipate along with our other primitive instincts once we moved out of caves and into civilization? What makes a civilian rush into a burning building to save a crying child? What makes a man donate a kidney to a total stranger? And what about other seemingly random yet selfless acts of kindness? Why does humanity choose to do good even when doing so goes against our own self-interests?

> Science cannot be used to justify discounting
> the great monotheistic religions of the world,
> which rest upon centuries of history, moral
> philosophy, and the powerful evidence
> provided by human altruism. It is the height
> of scientific hubris to claim otherwise.[6]
> —Francis Collins

Though Dawkins rightly catalogs religion's many deficiencies, he fudges or simply skips over virtues. On Beliefnet.com, Greg Easterbrooks observes, "Set aside whether or not God exists: it is beyond doubt that religion is at the core of much of the world's philanthropy."[7] Obviously, good deeds are done by secular humanists. The Bill & Melinda Gates Foundation and Doctors Without Borders prove that one need not follow a particular faith in order to better humanity. TheResurgence.com, an outgrowth of the teaching ministry of Mars Hill Church in Seattle, offers this observation by Ed Stetzer on their blog:

Do atheists give their lives to the poor for the love of Christ? I am sure some atheists do serve others and have a desire to help, but my experience reflects that many others do not. There are plenty of bad examples from Christians and non-Christians alike, but the list of atheists who have sacrificially given their lives to the poor is shorter than that of French war victories.[8]

MLK Moved Mountains

I've already touched on the fact that while the New Atheists run roughshod over religion's many deficiencies, they fudge or simply skip over the virtues. This is a subject that I'd like to tackle in more depth. What good exactly does religion do?

> For I was hungry and you gave me food,
> I was thirsty and you gave me drink;
> I was a stranger and you took Me in;
> I was sick and you visited Me;
> I was in prison and you came to Me.[9]
> —Jesus of Nazareth

In Dawkins's dissin' of the faith, he neglects the countless acts of good that have been done throughout history in the name of religion. For example, he pretty much blows off Martin Luther King Jr. Sorry, bud, but you can't dismiss this mighty man who was the spark that set the civil rights movement ablaze. Yes, King was human, not God, but that's true of all of us. (I can list my faults chronologically or alphabetically, depending upon your particular preference.) Still, his ongoing legacy demands that this righteous reverend be taken seriously.

Now, I wasn't even born when my dad and mom participated in the Woolworth Lunch Counter boycott in 1960, though I later read how other clergy participated in this historic sit-in. I was told years after my father's death that he was the only white clergyman who dared preach the need for desegregation in Hartsville, South Carolina, circa the late 1950s, an act that led to the Ku Klux Klan chasing him out of the state in 1962.[10] So, please don't tell me the civil rights movement wasn't connected to the Christian churches, 'cause it just ain't so.

Sam Harris admits, "Martin Luther King, to some significant degree, was animated by Christianity."[11] But then he does a complete U-turn to discount that any of Jesus' teaching on nonviolence had any impact whatsoever on Martin's moves.

When you look at why he preached nonviolence to the degree that he did, he didn't get that from Christianity. He got it from Mahatma Gandhi. And Gandhi got it from the Jains. Jainism is a religion of India that preaches this doctrine of nonviolence. To argue that that's the true face of Christianity is really misleading.[12]

Say what? If Jesus hadn't risen from the dead, He'd be turning around in His tomb right about now. What part about Jesus' teachings on nonviolence does Sammy here not understand?[13] Harris implies that King was jonesing for some Jainism, when in fact this spiritual leader was swimming in the words of the Old Testament and the gospel teachings of Jesus.

Here Harris cherry-picks through Gandhi's teachings; he conveniently chooses to overlook Gandhi's admission of how this peaceful pioneer was influenced by the teachings of Jesus and Leo Tolstoy's *The Kingdom of God Is Within You*.[14] According to Martin Luther King Jr.'s own admission, Tolstoy, Jesus, and Gandhi served as the models for his nonviolence actions.[15] How can anyone look at this trio and not conclude that Christianity played a pivotal role in King's understanding of his mission?

Now, I'm not dissin' Jainism, mind you. I never said Christianity has a monopoly on peace. It's just that we need to get the facts right here. Distorting history to make political points is a major no-no in my book. Simply put, you need to give credit where credit is due. In this case, King led a Bible-based nonviolence movement for racial equality.

Lest anyone still thinks King attended some secular humanist camp, sorry, but this dude was a definite Jesus jumper. He was a Baptist minister, steeped in the historic black church tradition embedded in the fabric of the Deep South. Do the research and you'll see the pivotal role that Dexter Avenue King Memorial Baptist Church played in launching the civil rights movement.[16] While many Southern religious leaders stood silently by, even Charlton Heston (aka Moses) joined Martin Luther King Jr. on August 28, 1963, at the "March on Washington for Jobs and Freedom, where King delivered his prophetic "I have a dream" speech calling for racial equality.[17]

How can anyone read King's writings and not conclude that this was a modern-day Moses, a prophet who was determined to take his people to the promised land? While obviously not everyone involved in this struggle was a person of faith, I have yet to see any evidence proving that this was a secularly inspired social justice campaign. No siree.

Furthermore, while Sam Harris assumes that Ghandi and King are exemplars (of their faith traditions), as Jean E. Barker observes on SFGate.com, he ignores that these twentieth-century leaders were successful because, in part, they refused to objectify their opponents, to settle for anger and hatred as the last word, to accept divisions between "us" and "them."[18] These aforementioned practitioners of nonviolence would deplore the stridency demonstrated by both religious fundamentalists and the New Atheists.

Human Rights Watch, an independent, nongovernmental organization dedicated to protecting the human rights of people around the world, acknowledges that in some countries like France, the human rights movement is tied to *laicité* (secularism) in an attempt to keep the Roman Catholic Church separate from the state. However, they note where history tells another story. "In other countries, religion was the prime mover behind campaigns for human rights. The role of US and English Protestant churches in the anti-slavery campaigns, in the Congo reform movement, and in solidarity with Armenian victims in the late days of the Ottoman Empire belong to the best chapters of the history of the human rights movement."[19] Other religiously inspired movements cited include Gandhi's long march for the liberation of India, the martyrdom of San Salvador Archbishop Oscar Arnulfo Romero, and the Roman Catholic Church's role in the Philippines during the 1980s to help overthrow the Marcos dictatorship. These are secular sorts we're talking about here. So if the Human Rights Watch, a nonreligious group, can champion the cause of religious freedom,[20] why can't the New Atheists do likewise?

Godly Justice

Another group visibly absent in New Atheist-themed literature is Jubilee 2000. Given how they like to hammer Christians for taking the Bible verses in Leviticus literally, why are they so silent when it comes to a universal religious push to put Leviticus 25 into action?[21] We're not talking some cheesy church supper, a half-baked bake sale, or a frozen chosen high tea social here. Rather, Jubilee 2000 represented a worldwide petition to achieve complete cancellation of unpayable and unfair loans made to third world countries. This is serious spiritual social justice stuff.[22]

Ron Sider, president of Evangelicals for Social Action, observes how this movement brought together "a highly unusual network of unlikely alliances: Puff Daddy and the pope; conservative Republican Senator Jesse Helms and rock star Bono; the Sisters of the Sacred Heart and the Spice Girls."[23] Given the amount of religious PR and celebrity glitter surrounding this ongoing, worldwide antipoverty initiative, how could anyone alive on this planet have missed this story?

Now, I admit, it's a hoot poking fun at priestly peccadilloes. But here, I gotta give the Vatican props for stepping into the ring and delivering some powerful punches in the global war against poverty. Given how much these anti-God guys slam the Roman Catholic Church, the very least they can do is give them an attaboy when they make a good-faith global effort to walk the walk.

Other faith-based organizations and initiatives not mentioned by these dudes include Bread for the World, Habitat for Humanity International, and Opportunity International. Yes, there are some faith-based missionary organizations that practice what can best be described as questionable outreach tactics. My heart goes out to anyone who has ever been at the receiving end of a bad Bible blitz. But I encourage anyone who thinks God is delusional or deadly to poke around a bit on the Web sites of the these organizations before you say the faith has fallen and it can't get up. I've barely scratched the spiritual surface here, believe me.

> It is a heresy, particularly common in rich
> nations, to think that wealth and prosperity
> are always a sure sign of righteousness. They
> may be the result of sin and oppression,
> as in the case of Israel. The crucial test is
> whether the prosperous are obeying God's
> command to bring justice to the oppressed.[24]
>
> —Ron Sider

Looks to me like an increasing number of Christians are passing Sider's test by getting back to the Bible basics. Glad to hear we're not all illiterates when it comes to the Good Book. Kewl.

Concurrent with this rise of New Atheism are the beginnings of new faith-based agendas. During his tenure in the White House, presidential speechwriter Michael Gerson observed how "the most intense and urgent evangelical activism I saw did not come on the expected values issues—though abortion and the traditional family weren't ignored—but on genocide, global AIDS, and human trafficking."[25] Purpose-driven überpastor Rick Warren proclaims, "The first reformation of the church five hundred years ago was about beliefs. This one is going to be about behavior. The first one was about creeds. This one is going to be about deeds. It is not going to be about what does the church believe, but about what is the church doing."[26]

Among the recent religious news to cross my desk are press releases announcing the formation of Evangelicals for Human Rights, the Evangelical Climate Initiative, and Evangelicals for Darfur.[27] Now, I'm not playing Polyanna here by any means. There are still plenty of evangelical excesses to keep me writing till the day I die. However, you gotta admit these positive faith-based initiatives represent a far cry from 1994, when the Ralph Reed Express drove the Christian Coalition's megachurch bus right through the halls of Congress, thus prompting me to pen "The Christian Coalition Congressional Prayer Primer."[28] Why these New Atheists can't see this spiritual-sea change is beyond me.

Their revisionist retelling of religious history makes me think there's far less objectivity here than one would expect coming from PhD-level philosophers and scientists. By discounting all the good done in God's name, they're failing abysmally to place historical events in their proper sociopolitical context. Isn't science a quest for truth?

CREATE IN ME
A CLEAN HEART

Are religions themselves a kind of saccharine for
the brain, less filling or debilitating or intoxicating
than the original and potentially harmful target? [1]

—DANIEL DENNETT

WELL, I DO REMEMBER THAT MY MOM LET ME EAT
my Easter candy during one of my dad's sermons so I wouldn't
hit my little brother and sister, thus wrecking the resurrection
story for the rest of the congregation. Then there was this whole
controversy here in New York City when an art gallery wanted
to display a nude, anatomically correct chocolate sculpture of
Jesus Christ during Holy Week. Thanks to William Donohue
and his band of Catholic League watchdogs, this "My Sweet
Lord" display got the axe. [2] But I suspect Dennett is taking a less
literal interpretation here.

Hmmm, lemme think about this whole relationship between
sugar and religion for a bit. Over the years, I've encountered my
share of spiritual junkies in search of their latest faith fix. Seems

they're always jumping for Jesus as though they believe that the faith journey can be defined as one massive holy high. They're the ones you see on the street corner or any religious event praising "The Lord" really loudly as they hand out brightly colored tracts targeted toward kindergarteners. If you're really lucky, they might give you a bit of homemade candy shaped in the form of a cross or some other delicious Christian-themed treat. Yippee.

In fact, back in the 1980s, I probably fit some of the criteria for being a religious addict.

I recall attending seminars, Cursillo retreats, a Campus Crusade adult Bible study,[3] and other spiritually enlightening events in search of the next "Jesus high." (I apologize to anyone who was on the receiving end of one of my prerecovery religious rants.)

As the charismatic movement in the US Episcopal Church took a hard turn towards the political right, I bolted the scene and headed straight for divinity school. By the time I left YDS, my faith had been challenged like nobody's business. I was forced to "grow up," spiritually speaking. Fortunately, thanks to spiritual saints like Mike Yaconelli, I never completely lost my childlike wonder and love of God.

I've left my share of clappy church services or praiseworthy retreats with one of those headaches you get from sipping a Slurpee way, way too fast.[4] So, yeah, I can attest: it's possible to get sugar shock from OD'ing on megachurch mania with all that glitz and gospel-lite content. Alas, some US-based "emergent" church leaders seem to think that if we unplug the power-praise band, chuck the laser light show for some candlelit "ambiance" and grow a goatee (this applies to the males only), then, voilá—you get this, like, wow, you know, buzz for Jesus, dude.

If a New Atheist or a serious seeker walked into these kinda services, I could understand full well why they would start searching for the nearest exit, 'cause I'd probably be right there behind them. This kind of canned Christianity makes me feel like I'm being manipulated to experience a spiritual high instead of having the music of, say, Jonny Baker or Isaac Everett transport me to a place where I can simply be and allow God's presence to enter.[5]

So, yeah, Dennett has a valid point here. Are we going to church for an invigorating workout of Jesus-cize and God gymnastics, or do we gather together so we can become empowered as the body of the risen Christ to go into the world and put the gospel into practice?

> Create in me a clean heart, O God,
> And renew a steadfast spirit within me.
> —Psalm 51:10

My first experiences of community in action took place in a church basement. These weren't church socials but Al-Anon and Adult Children of Alcoholic (ACOA) meetings.[6] Thanks to the support and teaching I received from largely anonymous souls, I was able to come to grips with the horrific and long-lasting effects that my late parents' alcoholism and drug use, coupled with the ongoing neglect from my extended family, were having on my daily life. "Our actual parent is a Higher Power whom some of us choose to call God. Although we had alcoholic parents, our Higher Power gave us the 12 Steps of Recovery."[7]

Based on my personal experience as well as those many stories I've encountered over the years, I've seen how a personal belief in God can encourage people to lead better lives. Through daily application of our faith, we can turn away from destructive and even deadly behavior and follow a spiritual path toward redemption, reconciliation, and renewal. So, I can attest to the healing powers of this spiritually based approach. Lest you think we're perfect, I freely confess that at least for me, recovery represents a lifelong journey.

Now, I'm not saying these programs are flawless. I agree with Dennett that some people replace their addiction to alcohol with their compulsive need to attend 12-step meetings. One can replace a deadly addiction with a less dangerous, though still unholistic and unhealthy, mechanism. There's also a limit to what one can expect from any kind of a mutual support system. I haven't participated in these groups since the early 1990s because there came a point where the words of Julian of Norwich, St. John of the Cross, and other ancient mystics started telling me I needed to leave the safety and comfort of these church basements and start walking along my own singular spiritual path. So, I went. But these 12-step programs were invaluable for helping me take my initial spiritual baby steps.

> It is left to professional skeptics to wonder
> how an intelligent person can believe that
> mere recovery from alcoholism
> confirms the doctrine of Christianity.[8]
> —Sam Harris

I'm not sure how much time Harris has spent around 12-step programs, but when I participated in Al-Anon and ACOA meetings, I don't recall anyone trying to "Christianize" me. Yes there are faith-based recovery organizations such as Christians in Recovery, Jewish Alcoholics, and Significant Others. But I just checked the latest AA-approved tracts, and I still don't see anything in any 12-step literature that follows the AA model that is explicitly Christian, or even religious, for that matter. In fact, I've seen how great care is taken in the AA-approved materials to distinguish between spiritual and religious experiences, with the emphasis clearly geared toward individual transformation as opposed to coerced religious conversion. For example, the twelfth and final step reads: "Having had a spiritual awakening as the result of these steps, we tried to carry this message to alcoholics, and to practice these principles in all our affairs."[9]

Show me where in the AA-approved literature the word *God* appears. In fact, the second step states: "[We] came to believe that a Power greater than ourselves could restore us to sanity." Some like myself knew this as God, while others use the more generic term "Higher Power."

> God grant me the serenity
> to accept the things I cannot change;
> courage to change the things I can;
> and wisdom to know the difference.
> —attributed to theologian Reinhold Niebuhr

Throughout the world, people come together in church basements, community centers, hospital conference rooms and other public places to utter this Serenity Prayer. While they come from disparate backgrounds, they're bonded together by the decision to turn their wills and their lives over to the care of God, as they understand this being. *The Big Book,* the basic text for Alcoholics Anonymous, professes "that if a mere code of morals or a better philosophy of life were sufficient to overcome alcoholism, many of us would have recovered long ago."[10]

While I know some addicts find help via other more secular methods such as Rational Recovery, why would so many people participate in a spiritually-based recovery program unless it was working for them? Given the anonymous nature of these meetings, one cannot get an exact count of how many spiritual souls have sought solace through this prayer, though Alcoholics Anonymous estimates that there are more than one hundred thousand groups and more than two million members in one hundred fifty countries.[11] And that's just the stats for AA. Factor in the worldwide participation in mutual support groups based on this model, such as Overeaters Anonymous, Narcotics Anonymous, Debtors Anonymous, and Al-Anon,[12] and the numbers of people working one of these 12-step program at any given time boggles the mind.

Along those lines, why would the *Journal of American Medicine* endorse these mutual support groups as a viable treatment offer if they were indeed bogus?[13] Seems to me if millions of people were indulging in a medically unsound regime, such as the Scientology detox program or the latest fad being promoted on daytime talk TV, the entire medical community would blow the whistle here.[14] I can hear the New Atheists chanting in the background that I'm making this too personal. Ya think? I don't see how else to talk about spiritual transformation except through story. Unfortunately, such stories are largely absent from the writings penned by these anti-God gurus. You don't hear names like John Newton when they start to rattle off the list of Almighty wrongs done in the name of God.

SAVED A WRETCH LIKE ME

The next time you sing "Amazing Grace," check out the fine print and you'll realize one of the most famous Christian hymns in history was penned by John Newton.

From what I've read, Newton sounds like a real piece of work. This rude and profane captain of an eighteenth-century slave ship experienced a great conversion while steering his ship through a storm. After becoming ordained in the Church of England, he eventually served as the pastor of St. Mary Woolnoth in London, where he developed a reputation as a fiery evangelical preacher. This church became a meeting point for abolitionists, including Wilber Wilberforce. And the rest, they say, is history.

Thanks to the movie *Amazing Grace*, William Wilberforce has been lifted out of obscurity and recognized as the great English statesman who waged a forty-year campaign to end the slave trade in Britain. Eric Metaxas reflects how "once this idea (of having a social conscience) was loosed upon the world, the world changed. Slavery and the slave trade would soon be largely abolished, but many lesser social evils would be abolished too.[15]

On February 28, 2007, more than five thousand churches in fifty states and ten provinces joined together to mark the two hundredth anniversary of the abolition of the slave trade, with a similar event occurring in the UK on March 22, 2007. Those gathered celebrated Amazing Grace Sunday by singing the classic hymn "Amazing Grace." Their collective voices created a powerful reminder that there are still twenty-seven million men, women, and children enslaved around the globe.[16]

What would the story of slavery be if John Newton had not found God? Had he remained a salty sea captain, he would not have been in a position to encourage Wilberforce to remain in politics so God could use him there.[17] Most importantly, Wilberforce's real redemption and justification were not accomplished during his lifetime or in the House of Commons. The greatest benefits of his work and toiling are still being realized when oppression is confronted today, racism is challenged everywhere, and a better, more loving world is ultimately created.[18]

Simply put, Newton's transformation didn't just turn his personal life around, but God working through him changed the entire course of history. In the forward to Jonathan Aitken's book *John Newton: From Disgrace to Amazing Grace*, Philip Yancey remarks, "Grace always has about it the scent of scandal."[19] John Newton, he adds, "joins the ranks of fallen biblical heroes including a murderer and adulterer (King David) and a traitor (the apostle Peter)."[20] Newton's tombstone reads, "John Newton, Clerk, once an infidel and libertine, a servant of slaves in Africa, was, by the rich mercy of our Lord and Savior Jesus Christ, preserved, restored, pardoned, and appointed to preach the faith he had long labored to destroy." What lasting legacy are these New Atheists leaving behind?

Then there's the story of the most famous sinner of them all, Saul of Tarsus. This soldier crucified Christians until that fateful day on the road to Damascus, when he encountered the risen Christ.[21] I can't debate the full scope of Pauline theology within the confines of this book. However, let's knock it off with this "Paul never existed" junk or I might have to run down to Duke Divinity School and sic Richard Hays on you. Trust me, you don't want this biblical giant to go all New Testament on ya.[22]

How many examples of the fallen that became faithful servants do I have to parade around before it starts to sink in that faith can be a viable vehicle for positive personal transformation?

GOD-FILLED VACUUM

According to Dawkins, "If the demise of God will leave a gap, different people will fill it in different ways. My way includes a good dose of science, the honest and systematic endeavor to find out the truth about the real world."[23] As expected, Tony Campolo begs to differ: "When the psychotherapists and psychiatrists have done all that they can to no avail, I believe that there is still 'a balm in Gilead' that can heal the troubled soul. That balm becomes available to me, when, in prayer, the Holy Spirit saturates my soul."[24]

Again, if Dawkins thinks this balm in Gilead is bogus, then to loosely paraphrase Britney Spears, that's his prerogative. But why try to take away from the faithful the very salve that saves them? On the Beliefnet.com Web site, Greg Easterbrook offers this reflective commentary: "Belief in God or higher purpose has brought millions of people to personal redemption—helping them turn away from sin, crime, mistreatment of themselves or others. Faith is a consolation during times of trial, and a comfort as death approaches."[25] Mike Yaconelli adds:

It is not that I don't believe that Jesus changes you, it is just that my definition of "change" has changed. Whatever the change is, it is not so much outward as it is inward. This difference that God makes is often visible only to God. . . . and no one else. It is a new way of looking at God, a new way of understanding God, an inner new-birth that liberates us not only from sin, but from our old way of viewing God. It is intimacy rather than ecstasy; it is seeing rather than speaking; it is loving rather than living; it is dancing rather than believing; it is silence rather than sentences; it is worship rather than wordship; it is playing rather than praying; it is yearning rather than conviction; it is faith characterized more by passion than belief.[26]

I got turned on to the concept of centering prayer back in the 1980s when someone gave me a copy of Basil Pennington's book *Centering Prayer*.[27] At first, the thought of sitting still and doing nothing didn't appeal to my highly verbal and hyperactive sensibilities. But over time, I learned to let go and let God just be with me. This technique worked for me until after 9/11, when becoming still was something I could no longer do. My daily way of life had become way too shaken up for me to just chill. A wise spiritual director suggested I do active praying by talking to God while I walked and worked. By following her sage advice, I was able to keep the lines of communication open. Eventually I was able to return back and center myself again, though I gotta admit, some days I'm still spinning out of focus.

New Atheist Sam Harris practices *Dzogchen*,[28] a form of Buddhism that strikes me as having many of the same characteristics of centering prayer. The key difference is that while I say the Jesus Prayer, "Lord Jesus, have mercy on me a sinner,"[29] I gather he thinks nonreligious thoughts. That's OK with me, but apparently he has issues with my meditation techniques. According to Harris's analysis of meditation, you're only allowed to travel to nirvana if you do it via the Sammy Steamer.[30] I fail to see what's genuinely reflective about Harris's decision to follow a spiritual practice toward personal serenity and enlightenment if he chides others who choose to seek solace through their own spiritual means.

Also, unlike Harris, my spiritual highs by and large come naturally. (I classify my collegiate daze days as extremely silly and not enlightening in the least). He admits that he came to this practice through the use of MDMA, better known as ecstasy.

Sounds like Harris is suggesting a return to that New Agey stuff that people dabbled in during the wacky world that was the eighties. Except for a crystallized few hangers-on hanging out at the Institute for Noetic Sciences, the Omega Institute for Holistic Studies, and Marianne Williamson's house, I think it's safe to say that we've all sobered up and moved on.

In fact, I'm noticing there's this huge underground push of people who are seeking a return to a radical form of spiritual simplicity. Alternatives for Simple Living, a nonprofit organization formed in 1973 as a protest against the commercialization of Christmas, equips people of faith to challenge consumerism, live justly, and celebrate responsibly. The appendix to *The Irresistible Revolution* also lists a host of local revolutions and ordinary radicals.[31] And this is just the beginning.

Ron Sider reflects, "In a God-centered biblical worldview,

persons, family, and God's creation matter more than money and unlimited material consumption. The scientific method, however, cannot measure love and joy in a family. But it can measure a growing bank account, larger cars, and increasingly sophisticated gadgets."[32] In the end, which matters more? Maybe I've been a starving satirist for too long, but in my worldview, I'll take praying for a clean heart over milking a cash cow any day of the week.

In the
Beginning . . .

Ironically, this [intelligent design] movement now
regards Dawkins as one of its greatest assets.
Why? Because his hysterical and dogmatic insistence
on the atheist implications of Darwinism is alienating
many potential supporters of the theory of evolution.[1]
—ALISTER MCGRATH, *THE DAWKINS DELUSION*

JUST SO WE ALL KNOW WHERE I STAND, LET ME come clean with my take on this whole teaching-evolution-in-the-public-school thingy. After all, these schoolyard fights seem to be the point where the rubber hits the road. Next thing you know, you got this creationist-versus-evolution monster truck rally invading the entire public school system like some cheesy B movie.

The religious battles have reached full-scale guerrilla warfare when it comes to teaching that man evolved from monkeys. Now, when I went to school, the creation-versus-evolution debate never really materialized, though the behavior of some of the high school athletes pretty much disproved Darwin's survival of the fittest theory. Again, I'm no scientist, but it seems to me that there is a limit to what scientific disciplines can objectively prove. When it comes to a question like "OK, so what started the universe?" I remember my science teachers telling us over and over again that while there are many theories, there is no universal consensus within the scientific community as to what started this whole ball rolling. At least for me, exposure to the flat-earth folks, creationists, and the intelligent design community have expanded my intellectual horizons. However, suggesting that perhaps we teach scientific theories in, say, science class, and then teach non-scientific but widely held views such as intelligent design in a history or social studies class tends to get both the PC police and the conservative Christian crowd up in arms.[2]

Unfortunately, compromise, dialogue, and discourse are not words heard from either extremist camp when discussing how life began. As a counterpoint to the Templeton Foundation's conferences that explore the relationship between science and religion,[3] The Science Network placed religion in its crosshairs and pulled the trigger. Their conference "Beyond Belief: Science, Religion, Reason, and Survival,"[4] rapidly escalated into an invigorating intellectual free-for-all caged death match that was described by anthropologist and fellow atheist Melvin Konner as a "den of vipers."[5] When assessing the content of the conference, Konner commented, "The viewpoints have run the gamut from A to B. Should we bash religion with a crowbar or only with a baseball bat?"[6] The ensuing conference carnage bore an eerie resemblance to a scene straight out of *Planet of the Apes*. One would hope that internationally renowned PhD-level scientists could refrain from trading reason for fisticuffs. But I guess not.

South Park creators Trey Parker and Matt Stone skewer with sacrilegious glee the sheer stupidity of such scientific stridency in a special two-part series titled aptly "Go God Go."[7] This convoluted plotline combines teaching evolution in the public schools, the childlike obsession over having to wait for the latest video game system, and Cartman's botched efforts to pull a Ted Williams and cryogenically freeze himself.[8] When Cartman is unfrozen in the year 2546, he learns that Dawkins and his wife, Mrs. Garrison, founded worldwide atheism. These anti-God battles rival if not exceed the worst religiously motivated atrocities of history. The episodes climax in a mock battle between the Unified Atheist League (a group "allegedly" founded by their cartoon version of Dawkins), the United Atheists League, and the Allied Atheist League over what to call their respective groups.

Is this twisted? You betcha. Is it also telling? Fur sure, fur sure. By substituting the words "science" and "logic" for "God," "Jesus," and "Christ" in phrases such as "Praise Science,"[9] "Oh Science, help us"[10] or my personal favorite, "Science H. Logic,"[11] Parker and Stone deftly demonstrate just how ridiculous both Christians and atheists appear whenever either group starts rattling off their jargon without first engaging their brains.

Daniel Sorrell reflects in *The Revealer* how this animated TV satire brings to life "that extremist enthusiasm for any belief system—in this case Dawkins's vaunted atheism and scientific rationality—can lead to sectarian group-think, absolutism, and even schismatic violence. Replacing religious dogma with atheistic dogma still leaves us with the problems of dogmatism."[12] According to Peter Rollins, "one can say that evolution and creationism are intimately joined together in their belief that reality is empirical, and thus in the view that the only good beliefs are those which are factual. In this sense people like Dawkins and Harris are profoundly religious in the fundamentalist sense. Hence, they're closer to their supposed enemies than they think they are."[13]

SHOOTING SACRED COWS

Not to worry. I am not one of the flat-earth folks trying to eradicate all forward thinking. But when these New Atheists show their true religious colors by viewing evolution (aka science) as their God, my satirical self starts getting antsy. Once you start worshiping a given discipline, now you're stepping on my turf. After all, shooting down false idols is what I do for a living.

As I begin my trek into Dawkins's sacred science sphere, I gotta confess that I'm a bit of a timid hunter. I'm not steeped in scientific training, as are Dawkins and Harris. I freely admit that I can't out-science the world's leading evolutionary biologist and a budding neuroscientist. Judging from their aggressive antics on the playground, they could easily beat me to a bloody pulp.

While these dudes have no problem in the pontification department, I don't profess to have expertise outside my particular field of study. So while Ann Coulter may play pretend scientist in *Godless: The Church of Liberalism*,[14] that's a rocky road I'd rather not travel. Besides, there's been more than enough material penned by both scientists and religious scholars along this whole Creationism-Intelligent Design-Evolution continuum. As a nonscientist, I don't see what I could add to the facts underlying the debate that hasn't already been uttered by one of the many scholars I quote throughout this book.

In my satirical quest to find common ground between science and religion, I found an unlikely companion in Stan Marsh from *South Park*.[15] When confronted with Dawkins and Mrs. Garrison's (no relation, I assure you) dogmatic teachings on evolution, Stan asks, "Couldn't evolution be the answer to how and not the answer to why?"[16] Bingo. Out of the mouth of a crudely drawn cartoon child comes the million-dollar question these scholarly, scientific sorts either can't or won't answer.

These ungodly bullies still haven't really explained their central claim that evolution is unguided and, thus, unorchestrated by any intelligent being. After all, Plantinga ponders, "Couldn't it be that God has directed and overseen the process of evolution?"[17] Kenneth R. Miller, biologist and author of *Finding Darwin's God* concurs: "A biologically static world would leave a Creator's creatures with neither freedom nor the independence required to exercise that freedom. In biological terms, evolution is the only way a Creator could have made us the creatures we are— free beings in a world of authentic and meaningful moral and spiritual choices."[18] Even fellow atheist Lewis Wolpert freely admits, "Not all of the scientific questions relating to evolution have been solved. On the contrary, the origin of life itself, the evolution of the miraculous cell in which all living beings evolved, is still poorly understood."[19]

Here's where Dawkins distorts the late astronomer Fred Hoyle's analogy that the probability of life arising on earth by purely natural means, without special divine aid, is less than the probability that a flightworthy Boeing 747 should be assembled by a hurricane roaring through a junkyard.[20] While Hoyle used this analogy to assert the role of the divine in creation, Dawkins takes this Boeing 747 and flies it into outer space. In a nutshell, Dawkins assumes that an infinite God has the same probability of existing as the construction of a material object from pure chaos. This, of course, assumes that God is made of matter and is thus earthbound. Hence, this analogy only works if one ascribes attributes to the Almighty that are just plain inaccurate.

Make sense? I didn't think so. Sounds like their sacred science cow may have gotten mad cow disease. Maybe it's time to just shoot the sucker and put it out of its misery.

Daniel Dennett confuses me even further when he tries to explain how our experiences evolve:

> You can not [sic] just learn from your own experience, but you can learn vicariously from the experience of everybody else. From people that you never met. From ancestors long dead. And human culture itself becomes a profound evolutionary force. That is what gives us an epistemological horizon and which is far, far greater than that of any other species. We are the only species that knows who we are, that knows that we have evolved. Our songs, art, books, and religious beliefs are all ultimately a product of evolutionary algorithms. Some find that thrilling, others depressing.[21]

I find I just don't get it. But maybe I'm just not Bright enough. Yes, I know I'm a product of my environment. Suffice to say, I've done enough family systems work that I can map out some pretty cool, as well as some really, really creepy components of my family tree. A quick romp through my lineage shows a preponderance of rebel ministers starting with Roger Williams. So no wonder I keep bucking the church. It's in my genes. Ever since this Yankee gal with an accent befitting a Southern debutante was born breech, I have always viewed life from a singular perspective. No question about it. And perhaps my love of the ocean is somehow tied to the fact that I'm related to John Howland, an indentured servant from the *Mayflower*, who is described in the ship's log as a lusty young man who fell into the sea.[22]

I know Dawkins dismisses Joan Roughgarden's use of biblical metaphors to ease her fellow Christians into accepting evolution as "bad poetry,"[23] but I found her insights immensely helpful as I dissected my rotting family tree. In *Evolution and Christian Faith*, this evolutionary biologist and admitted Christian makes the distinction between material and spiritual relationships. Citing Genesis 1:27, where in the image of God He created male and female, she draws the distinction that "we inherit our bodies from our ancestors who were also the ancestors of other species. We do not inherit our souls from ancestors."[24]

When Francis Collins remarks, "If God is outside of nature, then He is outside of space and time,"[25] the New Atheists start to sneer and glare as if they are ravenous wolves about to devour their prey. But they still haven't explained how this thing we call "life" got to earth in the first place. What was this first spark that set the whole earth spinning? Yes, nature presents us with many of God's wonders. But unlike these secular scientists, as I gaze upon a sunset or another display of God's gloriously gooey finger paintings, I choose to contemplate the One who created such magnificent handiwork. Why in God's name did He want to greet us each morning with a flaming yellow sunrise and then end the day with a brightly colored sunset? Beats me, but man, oh man, am I glad God gets off showing His glory like this.

I like to call the one who created me by name. God, YHWH, Abba, Father, the Almighty, Higher Power, and the Divine are just some of the many words used by people throughout the world for centuries to communicate with the one who created us.

For as long as I can remember, I've always connected to God through nature. As a little kid, I'd take long walks in the woods with my dog, Quicky, or hop on Lucky, the family pony, and ride off into my own natural Narnia. Even though I didn't talk to God per se, I see now where He was communicating directly to my child-like heart through Quicky and Lucky. He still speaks to me today, only this time I do a slightly better job of listening and responding.

In fact, even though I go to church on a semiregular basis, it's on the water where I truly worship. The forward and backward motion of fly casting or kayaking are akin to the Jesus Prayer[26] where I breathe in "Lord Jesus Christ, Son of the living God" and breathe out "Have mercy on me a sinner." I combine this ancient prayer and my love of the outdoors to create a meditative practice that is uniquely my own and how I connect to God. The water's always talked to me ever since I was a kid. My mom's side of the family has a place up at Prudence Island, Rhode Island. No matter what happened, the Narragansett Bay would say something to me, and somehow, I felt better. Rivers, lakes, and oceans are kind of like people. Each one has a unique personality—a slow brook trickling over my feet, a river moving faster than a freight train, savage waves slamming against a rocky beach, or the gentle ripples that form on a quiet lake. They're all different, and they're all saying something. But we're all too busy running around and acting busy to hear what's really going on. But if you listen, you'll learn plenty. Believe you me.

Right after my dad died, I went up to Prudence, and let's just say my family wasn't acting very supportive. As usual, they were all drunk and cracking rude jokes. Yeah, I was laughing, but mainly 'cause I didn't want to cry in front of them. But I went down to the ocean and bawled my eyes out, and the waves told me everything was going to be OK. Eleven months later, I was back up at Prudence, because my mom had just died. This time my family was acting even worse. They were actually blaming dad for killing mom, you know, dad being an alcoholic and all. Not the kind of stuff you tell someone who was just orphaned. But the ocean saved me, again telling me I was going to get through this. And I have. I'm starting to see why Jesus was a fisherman—makes sense to me.[27]

But I know the New Atheists are just going to dismiss my personal connections with God's good earth as goofy gibberish. At this point, I'd better bring in a much better brain than me.

Francis Collins offers this insightful reflection: "If God is outside of nature then science can neither prove nor disprove its existence."[28] Alister McGrath concurs, adding that "[Stephen Jay] Gould rightly insists that science can work only with naturalistic explanations; it can neither affirm nor deny the existence of God."[29]

OK, so let me see if I get this straight. Even these esteemed scientists note the absurdity of trying to use reason to define a God who is outside the realm of reason. Hmmm. Interesting. So to quote Mr. Spock (the character on *Star Trek*, not the baby doctor), these same scientists who ridicule religion appear to be illogical when it comes to matters of faith. Collins surmises their seemingly backwoods approach: "[atheism] must be considered a form of blind faith, in that it adopts a belief system that cannot be defended on the basis of pure reason."[30]

DUMBING DOWN THE DATA

As we move on to other unreasonable assumptions made by these New Atheist dudes, once again, I'm stumped. For reasons that escape me, they seem to apply an uncritical eye toward Darwin's biography. One of their major mantras is that Darwin was one of their atheist buds. However, this naturalist, who once considered the priesthood as a profession, was a lifelong member of St. Mary's in Downe, England. If you look over a timeline of Darwin's life, it appears he started to veer toward agnosticism following the death of his eleven-year-old daughter in 1851.[31]

Also, as evolutionary biologist David Sloan Wilson reported in his book *Evolution Is for Everyone*, "[Darwin's] interactions with people from all walks of life were primarily respectful and cordial. We can learn from his humility and good humor in presenting his theory to others, in addition to the theory itself."[32] Perhaps certain contemporary Darwinians could take a page from Darwin's playbook and follow not just his methodology but also his manners.

My theory of evolution is
that Darwin was adopted.[33]
—Stephen Wright

Labeling Darwin an atheist might help to prop up the spurious claim that all evolutionists worth their scientific salt are atheists. But just as I raised questions about Voltaire's lack of faith, I'm not prepared to concede that Darwin was a hard-core atheist. One could argue that these heavy hitters wrestled with many of the same questions about organized religion that have troubled thinkers throughout the ages.

Furthermore, aggressive atheists like Dawkins disprove God using medieval material such as Thomas Aquinas's cosmological and teleological arguments, and Anselm's ontological argument.[34] While Thomas and Anselm may be saints, our theological thinking has (*ahem*) evolved considerably since the Middle Ages. How about we agree to a truce? I won't refute the latest scientific discoveries by promoting, say, the use of leeches and other grotesque medieval medical practices if you delve into theologians who have, oh, I don't know . . . lived during the last hundred years! That might be a good start.

While we're discussing turning swords into plowshares, how about if we both agree not to pull out select biblical texts and hurl them at each other? Francis Collins is right on the money when he proclaims, "Despite twenty-five centuries of debate, it is fair to say that no human knows what the meaning of Genesis 1 and 2 was precisely intended to be."[35] New Testament professor Jeannine Brown adds, "While the Bible can be rightly understood as containing propositions, its communicative message is far broader."[36] At the risk of doing a major disservice to centuries of biblical criticism, in a nutshell, one can say that obtaining empirical evidence from a book including but not limited to narrative, poetry, epistle, apocalyptic literature and legal texts, clearly misses the meaning behind these messages.[37]

Let's reflect instead on the wisdom offered by N. T. Wright: "The Bible isn't there simply to be an accurate reference point for people who want to look things up and be sure they got them right. It is there to equip people to carry forth his purposes of new covenant and new creation."[38] Simon Conway Morris, professor of earth sciences at Cambridge University, concurs. "I think if you try and make the Bible into a quasi-scientific document, you're doing it great disservice, if not violence. And you're also distorting, if not maligning, science, which is an attempt to understand the world as we see it."[39]

JUST THE FACTS?

Yes, I agree there is some rather dubious and odious stuff trying to pass itself off as scientific literature. Biologist Kenneth Miller laments the lack of scientific knowledge here in the United States.

> Less than half the US population believes that humans evolved from an earlier species. The reason, I would argue, is not because they aren't aware of the strength of the scientific argument behind it. Instead, it is because of a well-founded belief that the concept of evolution is used routinely, in the intellectual sense, to justify and advance a philosophical worldview that they regard as hostile and even alien to their lives and values.[40]

As a start, I'd encourage the New Atheists to kindly refrain from referencing some of the creepier Christian literature as positive proof that we're all a buncha believing buffoons. That just dumbs down the debate. If you're going to throw tasteless tracts in my face, then how about I counter by singing songs from Schoolhouse Rock's *Science Rock* series at the top of my lungs?

I agree that the Watchtower Society's pamphlet *Life: How Did It Get Here? By Evolution or By Creation?*[41] is indeed scary stuff. I live in Manhattan and whenever I trek over to Brooklyn, I make sure to stay as far away as I can from the Watchtower building. Just about every Christian I know runs for the hills whenever the Jehovah's Witnesses come a-knockin'. They creep me out the same way I get the heebie-jeebies when I get a bit too close to clowns.

But if we want to support this whole separation-of-church-and-state thingy, then we have to accept the cold, hard fact that some really dubious material is gonna get printed. It's called free speech. Like it or not, this material is supported by the First Amendment. That doesn't mean you're required by law to pay attention to such religious rubbish. When I get heretical-sounding hooey like this handed to me, I've evolved to the point where I just smile and say thank you. Then, once the party is out of sight, I chuck it into the nearest trash receptacle. I also circular file the really bizarre-o anti-God material as well. Not that hard to do.

Please don't assume that just because someone buys into a position of faith, he loses all his natural skepticism and scientific credibility. John D. Caputo observes how thoughtful theologians carry on Socrates' mantra that "the unexamined life is not worth living": "Religious faith does not put questioning to sleep, but on the contrary, exposes the depth of our existence, releasing an endless chain of reflection and a lifelong search that starts out with a humble confession of how little we know."[42]

DEFENDING GOD'S HANDIWORK

If God is truly God, then why would He be threatened by science that makes ongoing discoveries about His creation? I don't think God really gives a holy hoot that somehow science will take over His turf.

So, when Sam Harris claims, "Francis Collins and Kenneth R. Miller are doing lasting harm to our discourse by the accommodations they have made to religious irrationality,"[43] one could flip the tables around and note how Harris hasn't exactly helped the cause of science by dissin' these dudes. I've spent enough time around academia to know that there are going to be rather intense debates among serious-minded scholars. It's understandable that someone who has spent the bulk of his life delving into a particular topic, will bristle when someone challenges his precious (and, at time, precarious) findings. We're talking about someone's life's work. No one wants to think that he slaved in a laboratory or library for years only to discover it's all been for naught. Add to this the nuances of the ego, tenure tracks, endowed professorships, coveted speaking gigs, the publish-or-perish mentality, as well as the other perks and pitfalls of the professorial lifestyle, and it's enough to make most academics act a bit asinine at times.

All too often the scholarly tone of the debate gets lost amid this derogatory static. Next thing you know, these boys start playing pranks on their opponents for reasons I just don't get. (Then again, I'm a girl, so perhaps some things are just beyond my ontological understanding.) Seems some wiseass whipper-snappers think that if they give their perceived enemy a couple of very public wedgies and get them to yell "Uncle," they will then recant their views.

Nah. Kicking dirt in people's faces just ends up with a total mud bath. When all's said and done, the last punch is thrown, and the last dude is dunked, these pernicious pranks just further antagonize one's adversaries. As expected, the funnier and more embarrassing clips end up being broadcast courtesy of *Fox News*, *The Daily Show with Jon Stewart*, and *YouTube*. But in the end, both sides end up looking completely ridiculous, and no one emerges as the real victor. I fail to see how such foolish frat-boy behavior will ever achieve anything besides humiliation and degradation to all involved.

I haven't seen any signs to date that this whole religion-and-science debate is going to die anytime soon. So, both sides better figure out how to get along somehow. If religion were merely failed science, it would have been supplanted by real science centuries ago. So why is religion thriving in the twenty-first century?[44]

There's the quest I want to pursue. Yes, I'm aware of this recent rash of publications on "the biology of belief" and the chemical processes involved in mystical experience.[45] But so far, these responses attempt to explain *how* humanity developed belief systems without addressing the question as to *why* we have this seemingly innate desire to connect with something outside of ourselves.

141

For thou hast made us for thyself and restless
is our heart until it comes to rest in thee.[46]
—St. Augustine, *Confessions*

Furthermore, this isn't an isolated individualistic pull, but rather a communal reaching out to God that's coming from the collective body of believers. Why do so many of us from all across the world possess the same innate need to connect to God, or at least some semblance of something outside of ourselves?

Our Unselfish Genes

Some inklings of an answer may be found in the ongoing work of Joan Roughgarden. In her view, "most evolutionary biologists are inclined to dismiss this selfish-gene metaphor as entertaining hyperbole."[47] She backs up this assertion with a new and, dare I say, unique wrinkle on this whole survival-of-the-fittest theory. First she suggests, "We begin by disputing the secular philosophy of our day that glorifies competition, the dog-eat-dog survival of the fittest, as excusable and even meritorious because such conduct supposedly expresses basic human nature."[48] Then she detects a flaw in this line of thinking, as scientists "need to understand and to publicize better the biology of animals with complex social systems in which organisms do not live as simple individuals but as members of social groups."[49]

Here she takes Richard Dawkins's selfish gene philosophy and turns it on its head. Dawkins may hold up a bird's nest as proof that robins are genetically endowed to make nests. But Roughgarden rides roughshod with her astute skills of observation. "The evolutionary success of a male and a female robin resides not in the genes they have as individuals but in the relationship they develop with each other. The conceptual problems that result from over-emphasizing individualism, and from the difficulties of defining what an 'individual' is, run throughout selfish-gene philosophy."[50]

Roughgarden observes how Dawkins's books (*The Selfish Gene*, *River out of Eden*, *Devil's Chaplain*, and *The Extended Phenotype*) develop a philosophy of universal selfishness as though that were a fundamental part of evolutionary biology. This philosophy not only goes far beyond the data of evolutionary biology, but it is incorrect as well.[51] Here Roughgarden roughs up Dawkins's genes a bit as she notes how this line of thinking "fails to appreciate the difficulty of disentangling the contribution of individual genes to the whole and about how a whole can function in ways beyond the sum of its parts."[52]

Using the example of cooking when flour, water, and heat produce a new compound (bread), Roughgarden explains how "when genes combine to make a body, the body becomes a unit more than the sum of the genes in it because the body now functions as a unit."[53] You can't separate the internal organs, muscles, bones, and all the other goo that constitutes a human body and create anything except one big mess.

Taking this analogy of interconnectedness one step further, Roughgarden brings up the apostle Paul's teaching on how we collectively become one body in Christ.[54] By one Spirit we were all baptized into one body.[55] Just as our eyes, feet, and other body parts play an integral role as part of the entire body, each one of us has a vital role to play as part of building up and maintaining the body of Christ. There are many members, yet one body.[56]

Hence, as Roughgarden proved poetically, this theme of a diverse community as one organic body, each part different from each other yet essential to the whole, runs throughout Saint Paul's theology as it does also through evolutionary biology and ecology today.[57] Now *there's* some interesting food for spiritual and scientific thought. Who's hungry?

PHYSICIAN, HEAL THYSELF

> Sam Harris: I'm noticing Christians doing
> terrible things explicitly for religious rea-
> sons—for instance, not funding [embryonic]
> stem-cell research. The motive is always
> paramount for me. No society in human his-
> tory has ever suffered because it has
> become too reasonable.
> Rick Warren: We're in exact agreement on
> that. I just happen to believe that Christianity
> saved reason.[1]

FIRST OFF, I NEED TO MAKE IT CLEAR THAT IT IS NOT
within the scope of this book to debate this entire sanctity-of-
life issue. Medical ethicists and theologians are already doing
due diligence in this arena. I discussed some of the dilemmas the
church is having regarding these life-altering decisions in *Red and
Blue God, Black and Blue Church*.[2]

Having said that, I concur with Harris and Warren's assertions
that atheists and people of faith need to have reasoned discussions
around the issues pertaining to medical ethics. Somewhere down

the road on the modernist interstate highway, humanity developed the tools to create and prolong life without giving equal and proper consideration to the theological and moral implications behind these newfangled technologies.

As we all travel along this tricky and rather rocky religious road, we need to be careful, or else this lively ride is going to make us all carsick. Francis Collins adds this cautionary tale to those traveling on the sanctity-of-life superhighway, "Anyone who portrays this issue as a simple battle between belief and atheism does a disservice to the complexity of the issues."[3]

Again, though I agree with Harris here, I have to question if he practices what he preaches. Harris's attack-dog debating moves just don't jive with what most civilized scholars would call reasoned discussion. Comments like, "Since 20 percent of all recognized pregnancies end in miscarriage, God is, quote, 'the most prolific abortionist of all,'"[4] show a profound lack of understanding or compassion toward issues of life and death.

Also, can the New Atheists please refrain from holding up Paul Hill whenever they need a believing boogeyman?[5] He is not the poster boy for the pro-life movement. Even Flip Benham, head of Operation Save America, denounced Paulie boy in my interview with him.[6] I'm not saying I bought into his shtick. After all, Flip flipped me off by refusing to admit that if he calls abortion doctors "murderers" on his Web site, then he bears some responsibility when some crazed Christian thinks this public pronouncement gives him a license to kill. Likewise, these New Atheists seem to be oblivious to the fact that their vitriol-laden rhetoric could well inspire some fringe fanatics to act on their hateful words.

We're not talking the movies here—this is real life with real people. C'mon guys. We gotta turn down the volume—lives are at stake.

GODLY MEDICINE

Will we turn our back on science because it is perceived as a threat to God, abandoning all the promise of advancing our understanding of nature and applying that to the alleviation of the suffering and betterment of humankind?[7]
—Francis Collins

As we wade through this whole religion-and-science quagmire, let us remember that according to moral law, the four ethical principles that undergird much of bioethics—respect for autonomy, justice, beneficence, and nonmaleficence[8]—are beliefs held alike by people of faith and those who do not profess a faith. Here I must part company with the New Atheists, as I can't buy into their overarching assumption that religion is not an effective repository for our ethical systems. Joan Roughgarden concurs: "My experience with ethical discussions taking place solely in a rationalist context without any system of values associated with them were inconclusive and seemed to be very open to manipulation, particularly motivation for the profit motive."[9]

That's not to say that anyone engaged in these kinds of debates should park their brains at the door. Just because someone claims an idea is inspired by God or science doesn't mean that scientists should accept said discovery without first subjecting the results to scientific scrutiny. Collins offers this sage counsel: "As we face challenging dilemmas wrought by science in the future, let us bring every right and noble tradition of the world, tried and proven true though the centuries, to the table. But let us not imagine that every individual interpretation of those great truths will be honorable."[10]

Baby Talk

Speaking of dishonorable fights, there are some super serious scientific smackdowns going on in research labs over the contents of itty-bitty petri dishes. Stem cell research represents this new frontier where the battle lines are being drawn with little space for wiggle room.

On one hand, you have those who believe that, thanks to the insights of neurobiology, we can prove that the soul is not an otherworldly concoction but a combo consisting of molecules, proteins, and enzymes. "Yes, we have a soul," says philosopher Dennett, "but it's made up of tiny robots."[11] And in this corner, you have those activists who proclaim that any use of stem cells whatsoever would be just dead wrong.[12]

When Sam Harris complains that religious leaders impede the cause of science by blocking funding for stem cell research, he makes a valid point.[13] Let's face it. Even though I'm sure many kids like me played with chemistry sets and entered science fairs, most of us aren't real scientists with degrees in a given scientific discipline. So, when we try to interpret the reams of data on a highly complicated topic such as stem cell research, we go into *Monty Python* Gumby mode and shout out, "My brain hurts."

Francis Collins adds this interesting food for thought:

> [Stem cell research] is very different in my mind, morally, than the union of sperm and egg. We do not in nature see somatic cell nuclear transfer occurring. This is a purely man-made event. And yet somehow we have attached to the product of that kind of activity the same moral status as the union of sperm and egg. I don't know quite how we got there.[14]

In the effort to craft a "family values" agenda, a host of highly complex medical issues were reduced to simplistic, spiritual sound bites. Anyone who is seen as thwarting this narrowly defined dogma gets threatened with a loss of financial backing and voting support come election day.[15] Meanwhile, many of these same "family values" folks think it's OK to fry sinners sitting on death row and tend to be the staunchest supporters of the Iraq War.

Just what does it mean to "support life"? If we as Christians believe that God is the Creator of life, doesn't this mean that life is a gift from this loving and gracious God? I am humbled by the thought that, wow, I'm here on this planet as a living and breathing person made in the image of God. Think about how mind-blowing that is. And when I say life, I am referring to the time between the moment we became a twinkle in our mother's eye until the second we draw our last breath.[16] Furthermore, when I say "we," I mean every human being that's breathing on this planet.

> We believe that all life is a sacred gift from
> God, and that public policies should reflect a
> consistent ethic of life—and address all the
> places where human life is threatened.[17]
> —Jim Wallis

> Give some attention to the distinction
> between killing blastocysts, as collateral
> damage in medical research.... and killing
> innocent men, women and children.[18]
> —Richard Dawkins

Unfortunately, these issues tend to be fought on the floor of Congress, amid the glare of the media spotlight, instead of in the halls of science. How do we keep the politicians, health care lobbyists, and others with vested financial interests in this outcome at bay, so that the scientists and theologians can help discern at what point humanity has stepped over the line in this whole creation-of-life continuum?[19]

Now, given that scientists and theologians aren't exactly nonpartisan, especially when their funding comes from some special-interest group with a very specific and narrowly defined ideology, just who should referee this lively free-for-all? Hey, don't look at me. I'm just a satirist, not a scientist or a scholar per se. So, don't expect me to have the answers. I'm simply raising the questions that we all should be asking, but for whatever reason, there's a code of silence here. That's all.

We haven't even hit the final frontier, a wilderness paved with custom-made clones. Now that we can clone sheep, there's considerable controversy as to whether or not cloning humans represents a Brave New World or the last vestiges of civilization. Along those lines, there doesn't seem to be any kind of a consensus over the ethics of genetically modifying embryos so one can order a designer baby that's disease-free, with a supersized IQ and a side of statuesque beauty. An examination of campus daily newspapers suggests just how much the DNA of an educated young woman who fits the requirements of the recipients might be worth.[20] We're talking big bucks here, with fees ranging from $12,000 to $50,000, provided one is under thirty, has the right body build, coloring, and SAT score. I kid you not.

The list of scary scenarios boggles my mind. Soon we might be able to do away with horror movies, because real life will be much scarier than anything the mind can conceive. Just because scientists can play God, does that mean they should?

IT'S MY LIFE?

As a social worker on the oncology floor of the West Haven Veterans Administration Hospital, I had to help patients deal with the dilemma of DNR (Do Not Resuscitate) orders. No, a DNR order isn't a death warrant, but sometimes science had exhausted all feasible options or the patient had said "enough is enough." Then I had to prepare that person to enter a hospice facility.

The Terry Schiavo international media circus demonstrated just how divided Christians are when it comes to determining the moment when our lives on earth end and, hopefully, our lives in heaven begin. This tragic case represents yet another dysfunctional family dynamic that had heartbreaking consequences.

Many Americans agree that this situation should have been handled privately by the family, in consultation with the medical profession and trusted spiritual leaders. But let's be honest here: it's unlikely that this case would have gotten national attention and requests for governmental intervention if Terri had been a non-caucasian who resided anywhere but Florida, the state where Baby Bush serves as governor. But given that Dubya owes his presidency to Jeb and the Religious Right, there's no way he could let this one slide. This case proves that conservative evangelicals are all gung ho when it comes to states' rights—except, of course, when they don't approve of what the state is doing.[21] The ensuing demonstrations also prove that Jesse Jackson and Al Sharpton will stop at nothing to create a self-righteous ruckus.

In this whole Floridian fracas, the debate over what it means to be a person never seemed to really surface. Clearly Terri had people who cared about her and wanted to keep her alive. Stanley Hauerwas reflects that when people are dying, "we seldom decide to treat or not to treat them because they have not yet passed some line that makes them a person or a non-person. Rather, we care or do not care for them because they are Uncle Charlie, or my father, or a good friend."[22]

When discussing the care and feeding of Terri, John F. Kavanaugh, SJ, professor of philosophy at St. Louis University, pondered the question of what exactly is human nourishment:

> When humans eat, it is as much about companionship as it is about refueling. It is about taste and savor, memory and refreshment. As for pegs and tubes, they are best used as emergency solutions to short-range problems. Unfortunately they have

become standards for nourishment, sometimes only prolonging the process of dying and often serving as a cost-saving way to provide nourishment without companionship.[23]

So, what options were available besides keeping her body running solely by machines or removing the feeding tube and thus starving her to death? Kavanaugh proposed removing her feeding tube in a manner so that her receptive family could give her swallowing therapy. However, suggestions such as these were lost in the religious roar of voices. The vast majority of the protestors seemed to be more concerned about maintaining their own street cred than being present with those closest to Terri, her family who was tangled up in the underbelly of a gut wrenching battle I wouldn't wish on my worst enemy.

Let us never assume that just because someone is bedridden and can't function unaided, it means it's time for her to meet her maker. I still have vivid recollections of a Christmas Eve service at Warm Springs Chapel, a small, white clapboard building located on the grounds of the Georgia Warm Springs Foundation, a hospital for polio patients. Because my dad served as one of the supply priests, we'd go up there every other week, and he'd do his ecclesiological exercises while I'd be thinking about the free luncheon buffet we'd all get afterwards.

On this particular night, right after my dad said the words of consecration, some bedridden patients were wheeled out on stretchers for communion. I was used to seeing a few patients wheel themselves in for communion, but that was the extent of my direct contact with those who called Warm Springs their final home. For the first time, I felt God touch my heart and speak to me. These people were in excruciating pain, yet they were grateful to be able to receive the Eucharist and my dysfunctional dad's blessing. For one brief moment, I saw my father as all that he used to be, the radical priest offering salvation to all, and not the self-absorbed drunk he had become.

Yeah, there's something out there that's greater than me, and for one evening, I could stop thinking about stupid earthly stuff, as I caught a glimpse of a world where there are more important things than if boys liked me and whether or not I was popular. There was something so much more significant going on. My preteen brain couldn't grasp what was happening around me, but my heart felt all tingly, and I knew, for one night at least, that God loves me.[24] My fellow brothers and sisters in Christ taught me a lesson I never would have learned if these bedridden saints were just discarded in a heap like yesterday's garbage.

God as Our Comforter

To ignore issues of faith is to ignore a pretty
fundamental part of all people's lives when
they're in the hospital, facing death.[25]
—David Shore, creator and writer, *House* (Fox Television Network)

During my summer stint as a hospital chaplain intern, I met my share of Dr. Gregory Houses who have no use for God in a hospital setting. Like House, these doctors sneered at me when I responded to a code as though somehow I thought their medicine wasn't enough.[26] In fact, during a harrowing night spent responding to twelve successful codes in the intensive care units, one smarty-pants resident reminded me that he was God. (The fact that all these patients died within the next twenty-four hours was not his concern, as he didn't lose one during his shift.) Fortunately, the wiser residents realized I was primarily there to comfort the family and the other patients who were understandably traumatized at the sight of watching a code in progress.

As about 80 percent of the patients were Catholic, I had to check the charts and make sure the person who was coding had been anointed. If necessary, I had to arrange for the on-call Catholic chaplain to come and perform last rites. Given the vast majority of the people who coded in the hospital were on their deathbeds, the survival rate of these codes was minimal. So, my prayers and the priest's holy oil didn't raise the dead. There was, however, a communal quality to these prayers that cannot be discounted. When I told their loved ones the person had been anointed and prayers were said for their soul, almost without exception I could see some of the anxiety drain from their faces.

One of my assignments was to cover the OB/GYN unit. The only time they called the chaplain was when a baby died and they needed someone to come and arrange for the burial of the body. At the family's request, I might also be asked to perform an emergency baptism.[27] OK, I confess. I have no clue about the efficacy of offering a sacrament to someone who is already dead. But I can say that these gestures provided some small measure of consolation to parents at a time of almost insurmountable loss.

In all honesty, I really don't empirically know what happens when I pray. In 2007, the Templeton Foundation released the reports of the largest study of third-party remote intercessory prayer.[28] The results suggested that remote prayer is not effective in reducing complications following heart surgery. Its use of the phrase "remote prayer" got me thinking a bit. I did a bit of digging and unearthed a study conducted at the Rush University Medical Center in Chicago, which suggested that loneliness could be a risk factor for developing Alzheimer's.[29] This begs the question as to how the patients' health in the Templeton study might have been affected if, instead of being given remote prayers, they were surrounded by a loving, supportive community?

Now, I am not suggesting that atheists are heartless, uncaring souls. Neither side has a monopoly when it comes to caring for those in need. I have been to enough churches to know that what passes for pastoral care can be pitiful as well. Nevertheless, I have seen that churches with vital ministries caring for the sick and aging in their parish seem to have a dynamic and flowing energy about them that's infectious. While the New Atheists like Dawkins can imply all they want that faith is a virus, I would love for the church to become contaminated with contagious cases of the "caring syndrome." I pray for the day when this type of faith virus infects all of our dead and dying churches until they become transformed into Jesus-centered communities.

A man who becomes conscious of
the responsibility he bears toward
a human being who affectionately waits
for him, or to an unfinished work, will
never be able to throw away his life.
He knows the "why" for his existence, and
will be able to bear almost any "how."[30]
—Viktor E. Frankl

I just happen to be drafting this chapter on Good Friday, the day Christians reflect on the crucifixion of Jesus of Nazareth. Coincidence? I think not. All too often Christians want to rush ahead to Easter when the altar guild and church musicians pull out all the stops. But before we partake of the Easter feast and sing "Alleluia He is Risen!," the rituals of Good Friday remind us that Christ had to actually die a physical death. The grittiness of that day grounds me by reminding me that, even in my darkest days, the future holds the promise of new life with the risen Christ.

RAPTURE READY?

A lot of them seem to think that the second coming
is around the corner— the idea that we're going
to have Armageddon anyway so it doesn't
make much difference. I find that to be socially
irresponsible on the highest order. It's scary.[1]

—DANIEL DENNETT

MAJOR DISCLAIMER: I WILL NOT DELVE INTO THE
messiness surrounding the "Revelation: Metaphor vs. Reality"
debate that has long divided the Christian community. Enough
books have been penned about pros and cons of Armageddon and
the Millennium that any interested reader can partake of these
Rapture revelations if they choose to do so. Besides, I'm armed
with my copy of *The Pocket Guide to the Apocalypse: The Official Field
Manual for the End of the World*.[2] So, if and when the Rapture hits, I'm
ready (assuming, of course, my white angel robe doesn't get too
dirty in the meantime).

I would try to explain all the various Rapture-ready theories
that have popped up over the years, but some of them are so far-
fetched I'd just laugh myself silly.[3] I do, however, need to touch
on what I would call Darby's Dealie, 'cause this seems to be the

theory that is getting the most press attention. For those who are not familiar with John Nelson Darby, this former Anglican priest and founder of the Plymouth Brethren propagated a new theology known as *dispensationalism*, which introduced a brand-new idea into evangelical theology: the Rapture.[4] Skim the Bible and you won't find the word *Rapture*, but you will find Darby's footprints all over the best-selling *Scofield Reference Bible* and the Left Behind series.

What's truly troubling about Darby's teaching on dispensationalism is that it eliminates from the picture any talk of the Beatitudes.[5] If one is solely focused on otherworldly things, then there is no point to working toward peace, social justice, the end of poverty, and the like, on the basis that such projects are futile. Add the influence of evangelical Zionists in the Middle East and it seems that some influential church members have definitely crossed that separation-of-church-and-state line.

As Richard Kearney points out, post 9/11, "Manifest Destiny was back with a purpose. There was much use of religious idioms of apocalypse and purification. Terms like 'sacrifice' and 'purge' were frequently heard."[6] He adds that "a major documentary on George W. Bush's apocalyptic mentality entitled *The Jesus Factor*, broadcast on *Frontline* in April 2004, confirmed that the President's evangelical relationship with Jesus was no longer a matter of personal salvation but a global battle between good and evil."[7]

Once the White House started preaching about Armageddon, the New Atheists along with many Christians went gaga. August Berkshire, vice president of Atheist Alliance International, reflects:

> Like hell, [the rapture] strikes atheists as a scare tactic to get
> people to believe through fear what they can't believe through

reason and evidence. There have been predictions that the world was going to end for centuries now. The question you might want to ask yourselves, if you're basing your religious beliefs on this, is how long you're willing to wait—what amount of time will convince you that the world is not going to end?[8]

> Many of these people are lunatics, but they
> are not the lunatic fringe. Some of them
> can actually get Karl Rove on the phone.[9]
> —Sam Harris

This singular focus on the book of Revelation at the expense of the rest of the New Testament lends credibility to Harris's outlandish claim that "as long as a Christian believes that only his baptized brethren will be saved on the Day of Judgment, he cannot possibly 'respect' the beliefs of others, for he knows that the flames of hell have been stoked by these very ideas and await their adherents even now."[10] As much as this saying makes us cringe, self-professed Christians like Ann Coulter preach, "If you really believe Christ died for your sins, nothing else really matters."[11]

I hate to admit this, but Coulter does espouse a commonly held belief that the whole purpose for buying into this faith biz is to secure the coveted one-way ticket to heaven on the Pearly Gates Express. When people who claim to be followers of Jesus spew such exclusionary self-centered slogans, they send a pretty strong signal to the rest of the world that all Christians care about is our own salvation, and to hell with everyone else.

What a difference it would be if our system of
morality were based on the bible instead of
the standards devised by cultural Christians.[12]
—William Wilberforce

My biggest fear with people who
call themselves evangelicals
sometimes is that there is smugness.[13]
—Jerry Jenkins, coauthor, the Left Behind series

A lot of Christians seem to enjoy betting on Pascal's wager.
For those of you like me who just aren't into gambling, Blaise
Pascal blended his two passions, mathematics and faith, to lay out
what has come to be known as Pascal's wager. It is rather simple:
it is smarter to bet that God exists, and to believe in Him, because
if it turns out that He is real, you win everything; if He is not real,
then you lose nothing. So why not take the leap of faith?

Can I propose a different wager? Rather than betting who
gets serenaded by a heavenly host of angels and who gets served
up at Satan's next sizzlin' sinners BBQ, what if we acted as though
the kingdom were here on earth? So instead of gating as the
gatekeepers to make sure everyone's all clean and tidy before
they're allowed to hang ten with God, why don't we all decide
to act as though Christ is with us today? I fail to see how putting Jesus' teachings into practice would have any adverse
effects, unless, of course, to those in power, 'cause if we open up
the spiritual floodgates, then they will have a lot to lose. But as
Shane and others have shown me, another world is possible. As
I understand this whole faith journey, looks like Christ is calling

all who follow Him to band together and really buy into this whole disciple biz until His coming again.[14]

When I say that Christ is with us, I don't mean in a cute, cuddly, "I got my own 'Personal Jesus' ringtone" kinda way. Such pallid public demonstrations of sickly sweet spirituality can give even the most faithful a massive tummy ache. I can only imagine how nauseating such Hallmark-y displays of commercialized Christianity must appear to someone who is questioning this whole God game. Why would anyone in his right mind want to follow such a banal, bubble-gum belief system? I know I wouldn't.

CARE FOR THE KINGDOM

Sam Harris captures the worst elements of this brand of crass Christianity when he laments, "This faith-based nihilism provides its adherents with absolutely no incentive to build a sustainable civilization—economically, environmentally or geopolitically."[15] Here Barbara Rossing, professor of New Testament at Lutheran School of Theology in Chicago reflects on the absurdity of putting all of one's eggs into a heavenly basket. "Raping the earth and justifying such behavior on the grounds that the earth is ours and it will be finished in seven years is like saying we might as well use drugs and abuse our bodies because we know we will soon be resurrected with new bodies."[16]

As Dr. Rossing reminds us, while the sensationalist and, in her words, "nutty" Left Behind books have grabbed the media spotlight and made the best-seller lists, their depiction of the bloody and violent end times differs from how scholars throughout history have interpreted this book. She notes how the refer-

ence to the word *earth* in the final chapter of the Bible is translated from the word *okumenï*, which means imperial violence. The
other words for earth, which are translated as *gaia* (dirt) and *cos-
mos* (world) are used when the biblical authors reference God's
creation. Using these translations of the word *earth*, Rossing illu-
minates how in Revelation chapters 17 and 18, it is the imperial
world that is destroyed at Jesus's Second Coming. She also cau-
tions that critique of imperial violence includes violence against
the world through our own neglect of God's creation.

If, as Rossing observes, the word *apocalypse* means "pulling
back the curtain," what do events like Hurricane Katrina, the war
in Iraq, and global warming reveal for us? How do we read those
signs as a people of faith to ensure that no one will be left behind?
According to Rossing, "The term prophecy doesn't mean predic-
tion. Rather, prophetic books such as the book of Revelation
serve as a wake-up call of what will transpire if humanity remains
oblivious to the telltale signs from God that something is amiss
in our world."[17]

In *The Secret Message of Jesus*, McLaren explores the dimen-
sions of this new world. According to McLaren, Jesus took up
and intensified the message of the Old Testament prophets
that a new world was not only possible, it was coming. "In that
new realm, evil in all its forms will be exposed, named, and
dealt with. In that new kingdom, justice, integrity, and peace
will overcome."[18] Stephen Shoemaker, author of *Being Christian
in an Almost Chosen Nation* adds, "When the kingdom of God
draws near—and it is always drawing near—it comes near in
judgment and mercy. It shows us God's dream for the world and it
reveals how far we've fallen from that ideal. And at this revela-

tory movement, it gives us a new chance to join in what God is doing."[19]

SERVE GOD, SAVE THE PLANET

If there is any moral precept shared
by people of all beliefs, it is that we
owe ourselves and future generations a
beautiful, rich and healthful environment.[20]
—Edward O. Wilson, *The Creation: An Appeal to Save Life on Earth*

McLaren keenly comments how Sam Harris, Richard Dawkins, and others have complained recently about the ways that religious people use sacred texts for violent and cruel purposes. He raises the biblical stories of Joseph, who warned Egypt of a coming drought that led to stockpiling of food, and Noah, who sought to preserve the species. In his environmental exegesis, McLaren reminds us how stories like these can fund our imaginations in more constructive ways, as we explore how to care for God's creation.[21]

Whether we hold the book of Genesis as the sourcebook for determining our relationship to this planet earth through the discipline of science or by some combination thereof, can't we agree to take care of this fragile earth, our one and only home? While there remains a seeming unfathomable chasm between the rapture-ready crowd and the New Atheists, I've found that the majority of people are genuine at heart. Like Spike Lee, they want to "do the right thing." But when faced with picking between these two strident sides, most Christians prefer to sit idly on the sidelines. And it's a pity, 'cause we need as many people as possible to get in the game and lift a hand to help humanity.

Edward O. Wilson reminds us how pastors and scientists "are both humanists in the broadest sense: human welfare is at the center of our thought."[22] He elaborates how part of the New Humanism is "an invitation to a common search for morally-based action in areas agreement can be reached. The tone of the New Atheists will only alienate important faith groups whose help is needed to solve the world's problems." Greg Epstein, humanist chaplain at Harvard University, concurs: "Humanism is not about erasing religion. It's an embracing philosophy."[23]

In Epstein's view, humanism needs to speak to the heart. He understands his position as Harvard's humanist chaplain as a mandate for organizing the millions of existing, to educate the world about humanism. Ideally, he wants to work with those from various faith traditions in a spirit of mutual cooperation and respect to help solve problems of the world, such as environmental concerns, human rights campaigns, and separation-of-church-and-state issues.

Where I've found considerable common ground with Epstein is that we've both witnessed ample evidence where both New Atheists and certain Christians have invested too much energy into converting the other instead of seeking out areas of cooperation. Also, we've both caught heat from our respective camps for our decision to build bridges and work to "respect the dignity of other beliefs." Hence, we'd both like to see more attention paid to cooperative acts of charity instead of engaging in Jerry-Springer style free-for-alls that all too often define twenty-first-century intellectual discourse.[24]

Epstein says that Christians have a responsibility to reach out to moderate humanists, 'cause by shunning those who want to work with them, they're playing into the hands of the angry atheists. According to CNN, recent research by the University of Minnesota identified atheists as the US's "most distrusted minority."[25] So how can we all move past our prejudices and our distrust of others so we can allow for a space to dialogue? Now, I can't speak for Greg, but I am not proposing a wishy-washy, anything-goes kind of dealie, where Christians park their faith at the door. However, it seems to me there's too much at stake for us not to start exploring the common areas of our humanity, so we can start to build bridges not bombs.

> For there is a commitment to the realization
> of human freedom and happiness in
> this life here and now and to a life of
> excellence, creativity, and fulfillment.[26]
> —Paul Kurtz, editor-in-chief, *Free Inquiry*

> There is indeed a need for a society to
> reflect on how it educates its children. Yet
> no case can be made for them to be
> force-fed Dawkins's favored dogmas and
> distortions. They need to be told, fairly and
> accurately, what Christianity actually teaches—
> rather than be subjected to the derisory
> misrepresentations of Christian theology
> that litter this piece of propaganda.[27]
> —Alister McGrath, *The Dawkins Delusion*

Conservative Christians have championed the idea that "the truth is intolerant". They shouldn't really be surprised to find atheists who share their views that intolerance is a virtue. One of the goals of *Off The Map*, a non-profit organization founded in 2000, is to make Christians kinder. One of the ways in which we believe conservative Christianity is broken is that it has made "being right" the most important thing; "being kind" is secondary. Adherents to this take the scriptural exhortation to speak the truth in love and subvert that into "If I am speaking the truth to someone, that is inherently a loving thing to do;" and conversely, "If I am not speaking the truth, then no matter how kind I am being, I am falling short of showing love to that other person.[28]

—Helen Mildenhall,
blog manager, Off The Map

WALKING THE WALK

> Christians seldom realize that much of the moral
> consideration for others which is apparently
> promoted by both the Old and New Testaments, was
> originally intended to apply only to a narrow defined
> in-group. "Love thy neighbor" didn't mean what we
> now think it means. It meant only "Love another Jew."[1]
>
> —RICHARD DAWKINS

I LAUGHED SO HARD WHEN I FIRST READ THIS THAT I'm surprised food didn't come out my nose. I'm so sorry for getting the giggles, but I just can't help myself.

Look, Dawkins is brilliant. No question about it. That is, of course, when it comes to science. But as Jonathan Luxmore, author of *Rethinking Christendom: Europe's Struggle for Christianity*, points out, "Brilliant as he may be in explicating biology for mass audiences, Dawkins goes badly astray when he ventures into moral speculation."[2] I think throughout this book I've demonstrated that Dawkins ain't no Scripture scholar. His runny religious ruminations should be taken with enough grains of salt to equal the body weight of Lot's wife.[3] This is the kind of sloppy exegesis that you might expect from some stoned-out seminarian who's so busy protesting and partying that his studies are "lacking." But I'm not talking about one of these dissertation-procrastination academic hangers-on. Dawkins possesses one of the greatest minds in evolutionary biology. So I gotta wonder what possessed him to leave his scholarship at home when he penned *The God Delusion*. Is this the best discourse a brain of this caliber can produce? C'mon.

But like it or not, the Christian community is just as capable of producing equally spiritually spineless scholarship. Whose idea was it to hire the Teletubbies to teach theology? Just because Jerry Falwell slammed on poor Tinky Winky for being gay doesn't mean we have to put affirmative action into over-drive and grant the little purple loser tenure.[4]

As I've noted throughout this book, whenever we Christians follow our own self-interests in lieu of living out the gospel, we play right into the hands of the New Atheists. I know I hammered on in *Red and Blue God, Black and Blue Church* about the need for Christians to make the Greatest Commandment numero uno in the political arena.[5] But this is something we really need to focus on if we're ever going to try and make this whole body-of-believers thingy work.

Believe me, I know full well how rough it is to put this commandment into practice. For example, right as I was in the midst of penning this book, I had a legitimate spat with some PhD boys who wouldn't let me play in their reindeer games.[6] Like Rudolph, my nose got all out of joint. So I sent out some lame-o e-mails that were anything but Christlike, complaining about how I had been excluded, mistreated, and so forth. Was I right? Yep. Was I being

Christlike? Nope. Unlike most of us, Jesus stuck to His Father's business and didn't seem to give a rip about establishing His street cred. But I can be a really whiney baby at times.

Fortunately, I have enough compassionate Christians around me who in their own ways remind me to get off my holy high horse. Thanks to these dudes and dudettes, I am slowly learning to be a follower of Jesus of Nazareth instead of just going through the motions as though I'm on some kind of a spiritual autopilot. Also, whenever I get too full of myself, something like the Tribeca Film Festival comes along. Having the opportunity to attend press screenings for documentaries like *The Devil Came on Horseback*, *Shame*, and *The Third Wave* really help me to find my way out of the faith forest so I can see the bigger picture.

> Take surprise out of faith and all that is
> left is dry and dead religion. Take away
> mystery from the gospel and all that is
> left is frozen and petrified dogma. Lose your
> awe of God and you are left with an
> impotent deity. Abandon astonishment and
> you are left with the meaningless piety.
> When religion is characterized by sameness,
> when faith is franchised, when the
> genuineness of our experience with God
> is evaluated by its similarities to others'
> faith then the uniqueness of God's people
> is dead and the church is lost.[7]
> —Mike Yaconelli

I found a real kindred spirit in Nadia Bolz-Weber, aka the Sarcastic Lutheran. Like me, she laments how "it's not easy to have my values (love, inclusively, grace) with my personality (sarcastic, judgmental, acerbic)."[8] Nadia and I freely admit this radical loving way of Christ is hard as hell to put into practice. If giving God your all and then loving others as you love yourself were easy, then we wouldn't be in this hateful mess we're in.

> Dear God, Some of your children are extremely irritating and, honestly, difficult to love. I don't really want to be around these people, but know that I am called to reflect your love to them. This is really gonna need to come from you. Pony up the extra measure if you don't mind, because I've got nothin'. Remind me that you, and not my personality, are my source, and that that is an endless source. AMEN[9]
>
> Nadia Bolz-Weber, *The Sarcastic Lutheran*

In *Simply Christian*, N. T. Wright provides contemporary Christians with a book that I predict will have the same enduring legacy as fellow Brit C. S. Lewis's *Mere Christianity*. "We are called to be people who learn to hear God's voice speaking today within the ancient text, and who become vessels of that living word in the world around us."[10]

I've already confessed that the times when I truly communicate with God tend to be when I'm on the water albeit fly-fishing, sailing, or kayaking. But I drag myself out of bed and come to church (or some semblance thereof), on at least a semi-regular basis, because I need to be in communion with fellow seekers. Together, we can reflect on how the Bible, as viewed through the lens of the risen Christ, can transform both our lives, as well as the world around us.

If more churches tried to put the Sarcastic Lutheran's prayer and N. T. Wright's reflections into practice, perhaps our Christian communities could better resemble wells of living water. Trying to look for Jesus in a faithful community of believers shouldn't be akin to finding Waldo. Brian McLaren reflects that "when Christianity sees itself more as a belief system or set of rituals for the select few and less as a way of daily life available to all, it loses the 'magic' of the kingdom."[11] Sounds like a pretty durn dull and dreary place to be, if you ask me.

Now, I have been in churches where I thought I was getting the Bible, but as it turns out all I was getting was a heaping pile of stinkin' Scripture scraps. Stunk up the sanctuary to high heaven.

I've sat through one too many sermons pulled from the front pages of the *New York Times* or the latest PBS special. If I want to get my sociopolitical fix, I can do that at home in my pajamas. And I can drink fair trade coffee at home.[12] I need a better reason than political posturing and social justice java to get me to stick around.

Then you have those pastors who preach from the Bible, but all too often they're performing what I would describe as cookbook Christianity. They pull from the Bible those recipes that fit their particular concept of salvation and then discard the rest of the good book.

In these churches, the recipe goes something like this: 1) accept Jesus Christ as your Lord and Savior; 2) get dunked; 3) follow this particular pastor's path; and then 4) maybe, just maybe, you might get lucky and end up on the right side of the

Pearly Gates. Now, 'cause you're all sinful souls, you're gonna backslide. But when that happens, just go back to the dunking bit ,and then rinse and repeat until your soul is so squeaky-clean you can see the light of Christ shining through. Then be extra careful to stay all clean and white, 'cause at any moment God could come and git ya. And Lord knows, you want to do whatever it takes to ensure your sacred spot up in heaven, 'cause if you die with the stain of sin on you, why, you're going straight to H-E-L-L (or "H-E-double toothpicks," if the pastor thinks swearing is a sin).

What these guys consider major no-no's will make just about anyone decide to give up on God. Heck, many straitlaced believers have told me ever since I was an itty-bitty kiddy that my destiny was gonna be dancin' with da devil. No way were they about to let me ride on their heavenly highway.

Now, what were my childhood spiritual sins, you might ask? Let's see. I went to a church where they drank wine on Sunday. My dad pranced around in a dress during church. (Well, he was wearing a cassock and surplice, so I guess he was justified, though his moves were clearly not sanctified in their eyes.) I wore pants. Sometimes we even danced in church, when Dad was doing supply work for an African-American congregation. The whole laundry list of sinful stuff that God is going to use against me in His heavenly courts goes on and on and on.

So, I understand full well what it's like to have Scripture slammed in your face instead of having the loving hand of God caress your tears. So-called Christians have discriminated against me for as long as I can remember. One example should suffice. In the winter of 1995, my grandfather was dying. Now, this wasn't your typical, run-of-the-mill, ninety-year-old grandfather going-to-meet-his-Maker mush. You see, Grandpa Roy was my last living parent. When he went, my brother, sister, and I would have no "family" home where we could go for the holidays. So I left a note with the Boston-based, high-society Episcopal church I was attending at the time, saying that my grandpa was dying and asking if they could please pray for him and for what's left of my family. (I chose this blue-blooded church because they had a very active young-adult group, and I still thought you could get decent dates via church circles.) Not only did no one call to see if I was OK, but I later got a bill from the stewardship committee demanding full payment on the rest of my pledge. Since the rector has left, I've been told they've cleaned up their act, so I'll let them lie in anonymity.

As you can see, I get why someone would walk into many "Christian" gatherings and then leave in disgust. I've done that shaking-my-head-in-shame thingy more times than I care to remember.

I know I've failed here miserably on numerous occasions to be the light of Christ unto the world. I just pray that those times when I let my temper get the better of me or said some snarky remark, I didn't turn someone off from Christ for good. Yes, we Christians don't always practice what we preach— we're human, and hence fallible, imperfect beings. But please don't interpret our bad behavior as ontological proof that God doesn't exist.

Throughout *The Secret Message of Jesus*, Brian McLaren unpacks for the reader how the real mystery of Jesus' scandalous message is how those who believe in Christ hear His teachings and then put his word into practice to implement God's kingdom here on earth. "In refusing to draw or respect racial, religious, moral, ethnic, economic, or class barriers, in welcoming non-Jews and treating them with kindness and respect, in eating with both Pharisees and the prostitutes hated by the Pharisees, Jesus showed his primal kingship with all people."[13]

The mystery to me is how in God's name anyone can participate in His kingdom if the church has set up such rigid church systems that make it almost impossible for any camel to go through the needle, as it were.[14] I've spent more than enough time inside the bowels of these country-club-exclusionary-type churches that I can state with Crystal Cathedral–clear certainty that by and large, these saintly saints tend to pull more *Caddyshack* than Christ-like moves.[15]

Something tells me if Jesus came back on earth, he wouldn't call Mary Magdalene "Muffy" and order his martinis shaken not stirred. Heck, the dude doesn't own the duds needed to pass the dress code required to gain entrance into the latest country club. Even though He has the best family tree of all, putting down on a chichi membership application two dudes as your dad, especially when one is a working-class carpenter and the other is the Lord of hosts, is liable to secure Jesus a one-way ticket to the closest inpatient psych ward. Call it a strong hunch.

A quick romp through religious history will show that there's been this ongoing desire to replace the kingdom of God with a worldly kingdom ever since Constantine converted to Christianity back in AD 312. So, I guess on one level, we shouldn't be too surprised that when religious folks get in cahoots with those in political power, you end up with such old-school-Hollywood-style epics as the Crusades, the Spanish Inquisition, and the Salem Witch Trials.

Seems too many of us are invested more in keeping God boxed in according to our human desires instead of allowing the fullness of God to enter our lives. But God is bigger than our limited humanity. He tends to find a way to bust loose, one way or another.

LIFE-CHANGING NEWS

Christianity is more a call to rebellion than
an insistence on narrow conformity, more
a challenge than a set of certainties.[16]
—E. J. Dionne Jr.

If Jesus' life, death, and resurrection are so life changing, then why is so much of the contemporary church so durn stuck in the mud? "For God so loved the world that He gave His only begotten Son, that whoever believes in Him should not perish but have everlasting life."[17] Even though Christian marketing tends to tack John 3:16 on every bit of merchandise they can find under the guise of selling it in a Christian bookstore, every time I reflect on that verse, I still get chills down my spine.[18]

It seems that throughout history, too many of us get invested in keeping God boxed in according to our human desires that we don't allow for the fullness of a God-lived life to take root and flourish. Until we start to live according to the gospel teachings of Christ, you can bet the New Atheists will continue to tease, taunt, and torment us. Frankly, who can blame them? Unless we're practicing what we're preaching, we're just shadowboxing. All show, no action.

Despite all these Christian fistfights that have disgraced the faith from the get-go, there have been many instances of the risen Christ's radical love breaking through all this Jesus junk so that the glory of God can shine through. Historian Richard W. Fox speculates that the "reason for the enduring popularity of Christian belief in America is so many Americans have known holy people who loved Christ so fully that they seemed to spend their days, in action as much as speech, 'just telling the love of Jesus.'"[19]

> At a minimum, the church should be known
> as the kind of community that makes it more
> possible, not less possible, to follow Jesus.[20]
> —Jim Wallis

The New Atheists seem to delight in highlighting enlightened Europe as full-fledged proof that a country can rid itself of religious trappings. According to their historical misinterpretation, if the rest of the G-8 countries can go godless, then why is America still living in the "theocratic Dark Ages"?[21] Sam Harris gloats with glee, "While you believe that bringing an end to religion is an impossible goal, it is important to realize that much of the developed world has already accomplished it. Norway, Iceland, Australia, Canada, Sweden, Switzerland, Belgium, Japan, the Netherlands, Denmark, and the United Kingdom are among the least religious societies on earth."[22] Using their illogic, all the United States citizenry has to do is buy into their anti-God game and then the entire world will be a peaceful world governed by reason, not religion.

Well, I hate to be the one that crashes their anti-Christian party, but Europe's getting God again. Big-time. I don't mean in a megachurch, megalomaniac kind of way, where the religious rhetoric comes blasting over the airwaves and into the political arena. But there's a definite sea change happening for sure.

According to the Center for the Study of Global Christianity, atheists are growing at 0.31 percent per annum per year (P.A.) (between 2000 and 2007) and evangelicals at 2.04 percent P.A.[23] Overall population growth is 1.2 percent P.A. In February 2007, Wolf Simson, editor of *Fridayfax2*, sent me the results from his "Status Report on Global Christianity."[24] He conveyed to me via e-mail that

> what Barrett has not done is having numbers on what he calls
> "the church you never knew," the amazing rise of underground,
> noninstitutional, DIY (do-it-yourself) communities of followers
> of Christ. In Europe he has reasons to believe that the growth
> rate of this form of followers of Jesus (a bit like early The Way)
> in EU and US is around 30 to 50 percent, the biggest growth
> sector in, if you wish, the "religious market." He would place
> the number of house churches (simple, organic, you name it) in
> the US at between thirty and fifty thousand, and in the EU
> maybe five thousand, and will firmly expect this number to rise
> around 30 percent or more by 2008."[25]

Now, as I noted in the previous chapter, atheists don't feel they are exactly welcome members of society. Hence the number of professed atheists is probably underreported. But then again, I continue to hear stories from small pockets of people who want to follow Jesus but don't want to call themselves Christian because of the baggage associated with this label, and in light of this ongoing battle to regain the political and religious Christian soul of America. Blah, blah, blah. Sorry, but this debate is getting a bit old, and it's starting to really bore me to tears. So let's move on, 'cause there's some really cool Christian stuff happening just below the radar.

Yes, one can quibble with the methodology of gathering data on any underground movement. But log on to the Web site zoecarnate.com,[26] and it's clear there are thousands of house churches' online connection points and other subterranean expressions of faith located around the world that so far fly below the radar of the established church. Mike Morrell, journalist and zoecarnate.com's webmaster, offers this reflection.

> Since I myself left more institutionalized forms of faith nearly a decade ago for uncharted spiritual waters, I've found that highly-committed-but-alternative expressions of faith have grown exponentially. Call them "house," "simple," or "organic" church, these open-source, egalitarian, hands-on participatory, ecclesiastical communities are providing a safe place for many people to thoroughly reassess religious belief and practice. Our house churches are often the last stop for disenfranchised agnostics who are considering a complete exit from Christian faith. Many times they find that their real beef isn't with God, but with the way religion often construes God—ironically, by returning to biblical texts and more radical streams of church history, personal affirmation of a loving God revealed in Jesus

is an easy recovery. I'm sometimes surprised to find that I res-
onate so much with atheist critiques of the contemporary
religious milieu—I probably agree with 80 percent of what I
hear. I'm like, "If that's atheism, count me in! I don't believe in
that God either!" And people like this, I've found, are more
open to worship, sharing, and divine engagement in a living
room than an elaborate religious building, which can be
intimidating and carry a lot of baggage. But I don't want to be
simplistic or romanticized. We have our problems in house
churches too, and sometimes people enter our lives only to go
ahead and become atheists or members of some nontheistic
faith. And they're completely free to do so.[27]

Looks like while an increasing number of people are choosing not to follow the whims of a particular denomination, there
does seem to be this hunger to follow the way of Jesus. Cheryl
Lawrie, who works with an alternative worship project in the
Uniting Church of Australia, offers these insights:

Many Gen X and Y-ers find the doctrines that denominations
tie faith up with to be irrelevant, but they have a hunger for
justice, for wholeness, for a different kind of world. And there
seems to be an intuitive knowledge at least a yearning that if
they live in that way, they might encounter some divine hope,
justice, or peace that lies beyond themselves."[28]

Brian McLaren reflects how those who choose to partake of this
mystery seek to engage in "living in an interactive relationship
with God and others as a daily way of life.[29]

So, yes, Sam Harris is half right. Religion when defined by denominational modernity does appear to be on its last legs. However, something is in the air, as the Spirit is definitely moving in some very unique ways. For starters, head over to Greenbelt UK, an international arts and music festival started in 1974 that currently attracts close to twenty thousand people each year. This ain't Woodstock circa 1972 or some leftover band of hippie Jesus freaks. No siree. As Greenbelt patron Rowan Williams reflects, "Greenbelt is part of my mental furniture." And this is the archbishop of Canterbury talking—you know, the head of the worldwide Anglican Communion.

When I interviewed Phyllis Tickle for *Rising from the Ashes: Rethinking Church*, she reflected on the seismic changes she sees occurring in contemporary Christianity. "Evangelicalism has lost much of its credibility and much of its spiritual energy as of late, in much the same way that mainline Protestantism has."[30] Lest anyone find this news so depressing they want to run for cover, Phyllis offers some much needed historical and hopeful perspective. "About every five hundred years, the church feels compelled to have a giant rummage sale."[31] During the last such upheaval, the reat Reformation of five hundred years ago, Protestantism took over hegemony. But Roman Catholicism did not die. It just had to drop back and reconfigure. Each time a rummage sale has happened, in other words, whatever held pride of place simply gets broken apart into smaller pieces, and then it picks itself up and to use Diana Butler Bass's term, "re-traditions."

As I ride along the religious superhighway, I find I need some new tools to help me navigate this process. An enlightening and dare I say revolutionary retelling of the gospel hit my desk a few years ago, when I was asked to take a look at Rob Lacey's interactive book and accompanying CD *The Word on the Street*.[32] More recently, I caught wind of Tickle's radical yet totally orthodox retelling of the gospel. In *The Words of Jesus: A Gospel of the Sayings of Our Lord with Reflections by Phyllis Tickle*, she categorizes the sayings of Jesus into five categories: Public Teachings, Private Instructions, Healing Dialogues, Intimate Conversations, and the Post-Resurrection Encounters.

> Psychologists have demonstrated many times over that what we say is tailored to and informed by the audience to whom we say it. In a sense, in other words, while each of us may be an integer, we have various configurations or arrangements of our "self" that we modify, exchange, and employ according to our perception of those whom we are at any given moment engaging. Jesus of Nazareth, being fully human, followed that same pattern, though once again I had never perceived or even entertained such a possibility until I began listening to Him shift emphases, adapt rhetoric, and fashion varying modes of analogy to fit those with whom He was speaking.[33]

Thanks to Lacey's latest and, unfortunately, last book, *The Liberator* (a revolutionary retelling of the New Testament), the *Inspired by the Bible Experience: New Testament* audio CD (nothing says "Oh my God" like Samuel L. Jackson channeling the voice of the Almighty), and Tickle's commentary,[34] I've been immersed in Scripture from some rather unique vantage points. Over the past year, instead of trying to memorize Scripture and verse—something Episcopalians really suck at doing anyway—I'm allowing these sweet holy words to fall on my ears and into my mouth. It's like I'm falling in love with Jesus all over again. Trust me, as much as I love Greek literature, I just can't have this kind of a relationship with any pagan god.

The bulk of this book was written during the forty days of Lent and Holy Week, when Christians take time to reflect on the final days of Christ's earthly life and how, through Christ, the triune God literally changed the world. Every year I go off in search of Jesus amid the spectacle that has become Easter, complete with the bunnies, bonnets, biblical bravado, and other silly trappings that have reduced the resurrection to a one-day festive holiday.

This year, I found myself reflecting on Peter Rollins's observation that "God is not a theoretical problem to somehow resolve but rather a mystery to be participated in."[35] And participate I did. Big-time. I prayed, sang, wept, walked, danced, listened, slept (sorry, it was a long week), and just stood still and meditated. (If anyone knows me, I'm sure they're laughing at the sight of me all still and silent, but trust me, I can do it. How else do you think I'm able to hunker down at the laptop and meet my writing deadlines? But I digress.)

My Easter Week started off with Palm Sunday, the day Jesus came in and did His donkey business I participated in a processional at Advent Lutheran Church on the Upper West Side. Some of our liturgies, such as putting black ash on our foreheads and carrying dead palm leaves around to Sunday brunch, must look bizarre to those who aren't part of the Christian tradition. But if they peeked in to Advent's open doors, I hope they noticed that, while the service was very traditional in tone, this multicultural crowd was not what one would expect to see in a Lutheran congregation.

Later that evening, I hopped over to the East Side for an alternative Palm Sunday titled, appropriately, Sanctuary.[36] The music of Depeche Mode rocked the house, reminding us all that we have a personal Jesus who is so encompassing and inclusive that artists ranging from Marilyn Manson to Johnny Cash have given their unique spin to this alternative punk anthem. A side of me was wondering if they'd bring out "They Ain't Making Jews Like Jesus Anymore," "Kooler Than Jesus," or my personal favorite, "Jesus Loves Me (but He Can't Stand You)," but maybe some songs just don't belong in a church setting.

On Maundy Thursday, I reflected on Jesus' last night on earth as a retired Lutheran bishop washed my feet at Advent Lutheran Church. When he asked that my writing ministry be blessed, it was as if a lightning bolt jolted me back to reality. By this time my mind was so fried that I was thinking more in terms of meeting demanding deadlines than of doing any kind of a dynamic ministry. Thank God he came along to help me refocus my energies and keep my eye on the real prize.

Come Good Friday, I chose to soak in the blues as performed by Broadway musicians at St. Mark's Church in-the-Bowery. Afterwards, I trekked uptown to an interactive Stations of the Cross over at Sanctuary. As I touched and felt each station, this journey to Golgotha took on a real visceral kick-in-the-gut kind of a vibe. When I nailed my sin of "anger" to the cross, I struck a small but potent blow at one of the major stumbling blocks that prevents me from walking fully in Christ.

Next it's high church holy season, as the Easter vigil at the

Cathedral of St. John the Divine banged out a full-blown bells-and-smells mass, thus ushering in this transition from death into new life. I actually have a few friends there, so an occasional visit has become akin to a grown child visiting a familiar vacation spot every great once in a while.

Saturday night was just the start of the "He Is Risen" trilogy. The next morning, I got up to partake of a multicultural first communion class held at Advent Lutheran and a really fun brunch. Then it was down to Easter at Avalon (formerly the Limelight) for another rocking rendition of "Personal Jesus." Through the eyes of Tracy Quan and the women of PONY (Prostitutes of New York), I saw Mary Magdalene redeemed from her status as an alleged fallen woman to the place of honor as the first person to see the risen Lord.[37] On Easter Sunday, a crowd of about two hundred people, many of whom had never stepped inside of a "church" before felt surrounded by a community of people who demonstrated the unconditional love of the risen Christ.

As we all seek what it means to be the church in the twenty-first century, I'd love to take the New Atheists along for the ride. Maybe then they can see that we're not black-and-white, cookie cutter, stereotypical Christians. Rather, we're a living, breathing body that, despite our earthly infirmities, seeks to be the embodiment of Christ here on earth.

Kester Brewin, author of *Signs of Emergence*, reminds me that this viral, powerless, bottom-up Christianity "begins on Good Friday, with the crucifixion of the temple-bound, profiteering God, the end-game of the Babel-onian plot of human power against divine love . . . But love will not be played with. She appears to wither, and then spring again, eternal. That's the spirit of Christ that many of us have fallen in love with and desire to follow. For we know that in this marriage, we will be together not until death do us part, but for all of eternity."[38]

Here I join Mike Yaconelli in sounding the clarion call that

the tame God of relevance be replaced by the God whose very presence shatters our egos into dust, burns our sin into ashes, and strips us naked to reveal the real person within. The church needs to become a gloriously dangerous place where nothing is safe in God's presence except us. Nothing—including our plans, our agendas, our priorities, our politics, our money, our security, our comfort, our possessions, our needs.[39]

If we truly follow this radical love-making, rule-breaking, life-taking Christ, then that's a party that even the New Atheists may choose to crash—even if it's only to sample the wine from the wedding feast at Cana that's being poured into new wine-skins.[40] I'll drink to that. Cheers.

EPILOGUE

AFTER I TURNED IN MY FIRST DRAFT FOR THIS BOOK, I attended the taping for the first ever *Nightline Face Off*.[1] In this premiere episode, taped at Calvary Baptist Church in New York City, *The Way of the Master* cohosts Kirk Cameron and Ray Comfort debated the existence of God with the Rational Response Squad (RRS).

In the Christian corner, Ray Comfort claimed he could prove the existence of God scientifically without resorting to faith. If there is a design, he said, there must be a designer, because you can identify the individual who designed items such as buildings, paintings, and cars. That argument was refuted by the RRS, the A-team, who noted that if creation needs a creator, then what created God?

Throughout the matchup, well-worn arguments such as "We're all atheists when it comes to Zeus or Apollo" and "Jesus never existed" were thrown about in a feeble attempt to disprove God. One would think an internationally renowned news outlet such as ABC News could produce a credible line-up without resorting to such minor-league players. But I guess not.

Watching these teams of nonscientists try to explain evolution versus intelligent design proved to be laughable at best. My favorite bit had to be when Kirk Cameron disputed evolution by showing pictures of a crock-a-duck and other nonexistent creatures that he claims proves evolution to be a fallacy.

Even though the atheists failed to prove beyond a reasonable doubt that God could not have been the spark that set all of creation, they seemed to have nailed the debate when Kirk Cameron played the "get out of hell" card. Simply put: "What you believe about God will determine where you spend eternity." At this point, if I wasn't covering this event, I would have crawled out of the church in shame. While this was supposed to be an ABC news program, I felt like I had entered a lame taping of *Saturday Night Live* instead. I honestly feared that at any moment Cameron was going to demonstrate the Church Lady's Superiority Dance.

I wish I could say these extremist encounters are few and far between, but the animosity on both sides of the God debate seems to be hitting a fever pitch. When I skim the slew of material refuting these strident New Atheists, I'm struck by how many people of faith are betting on Pascal's wager. According to this logic, one should believe in God as a safeguard to avoid spending eternity surrounded by the flames of hell. The overarching emphasis here seems to be on the personal nature of Christianity as a means of guaranteeing one an eternal night's sleep, with scant attention being paid to what it means to implement Jesus' teachings here on earth.

Still, I see glimmers of hope. For example, prior to going to this taping, I sat in on a panel that was part of the Tribeca Film Festival, titled "Prodigies, Nobelists and Penguins: Science and Stereotypes in the Movies."[2] Here, I found a group of film-makers and scientists who were open to exploring where we can find common ground between religion and science.

I can't speak for the atheists, but for those of us who profess to follow Jesus, do we dare create spaces where we can dialogue with others who aren't like us, or are we so concerned about being right that we forget what it means to put Christ's teachings into practice?[3] I pray we have the wisdom and the courage to live out the truth of a Christ-filled life, for that's the love that will in the end conquer all. Amen.

ACKNOWLEDGMENTS

THE FOLKS I THANKED IN THE ACKNOWLEDG-ments for *Red and Blue God, Black and Blue Church* deserve another round of applause for sticking with me and keeping me honest. A special thanks goes out to Greg Daniel for convincing me to write this book, as well as everyone at Thomas Nelson who helped make this project a reality. Kudos also to Mike Morrell for proofing this sucker. And a real shout out to everyone on my e-mail list who keeps me sane and connected during my deadlines—you know who you are, and God bless you.

Appendix A

500 BC   Diagoras of Melos, the "first atheist" is blasphemed, leading the way for Socrates to take a hemlock hit for the all-Atheist A-team.

AD 1   A myth is born. As it turns out, monks miscalculated the date, so this myth was probably born on another date. Go figure.

29   A myth refuses to die. Once again, these mythmakers can't even get their dates right.

64   Great fire in Rome. Just blame the dog or the Christians. Same thing.

394   The Romans give street cred to this bogus myth by making it the official religion of the Roman Empire.

1095–1291   The Crusades. There goes the neighborhood.

1478   The Spanish Inquisition hosts a very unkosher BBQ.

1500s   The term *athéisme* is coined in France. It is initially used as an accusation against scientists, critics of religion, materialistic philosophers, deists, and others who seemed to represent a threat to established beliefs. *Oui, oui, oui.*

1616 According to eyewitness atheist accounts, the Catholic Church goes all medieval on Galileo Galilei.

1692 The Salem Witch trials begin in Massachusetts. Fry the faithful!

1776 David Hume dies a faithful death.

1858 Edgardo Mortara is kidnapped from his home in a very unkosher move.

1879 Fall of the Bastille. *Sacré bleu!*

1883 Karl Marx dies allegedly from a religiously induced opiate overdose.

1900 Friedrich Nietzsche is dead and, whaddaya know, so is God!

1915 Former Methodist minister William J. Simmons revitalizes the Ku Klux Klan and introduces the practice of cross-burning.

1925 Scopes Monkey Trial causes devolution among fundamentalists.

1927 With the publication of *The Future of an Illusion*, Sigmund Freud compares religion to a child neurosis. Also, Bertrand Russell delivers his lecture "Why I Am Not a Christian" to the National Secular Society, South London Branch, at Battersea Town Hall. Bert and Sig, they're our men! If they can't hate God, nobody can!

1933 Hitler appointed chancellor of Germany. Heresy happens.

1941	Richard Dawkins brought forth into the world. All Hail Science!
1942	Daniel Dennett breaks the spell and is born.
1954	The words "under God" are inserted into the US Pledge of Allegiance. Atheists are now declared to be unpatriotic.
1955	Westboro Baptist Church is established by Pastor Fred Phelps, thus proving that God hates homosexuals.
1956	The national motto on US coins is changed from *E Pluribus Unum* to *In God We Trust*. Atheists no longer trust money.
1956	Ayn Rand cashes in, thanks to *Atlas Shrugged*. You Go anti-God girl!
1960	*Elmer Gantry* is released as a major motion picture. Praise the Lord and pass the offering plate.
1960	Madalyn Murray (later O'Hair) raises holy hell about public prayer in the schools.
1966	John Lennon declares that the Beatles are more popular than Jesus.
1967	Sam Harris's birth signifies the end of faith.
1968	People say the Death of God movement dies, but we all know it's just resting.
1976	Dawkins's book *The Selfish Gene* introduces the term *memes* into the atheist lexicon. Memes madness begins.
1978	The Freedom From Religion Foundation (FFRF) is established. Let freedom ring!

1979   In response to FFRF, Jerry Falwell does a back-wards flip and founds the Moral Majority.

1987   Religious hypocrisy hits prime time big-time when (1) Oral Roberts claims that God will "call him home" if he is unable to raise $8 million; (2) Jim Bakker admits to adultery; resigns from the PTL; and (3) Pat Robertson announces that God has anointed him to be president of the United States. Thanks be to science!

1987   While campaigning for the presidency, George H. W. Bush claims atheists should not be considered citizens or patriots of the United States. *Vive la France!*

1989   The Berlin Wall comes tumbling down. There goes the neighborhood again.

1993   The Roman Catholic Church in the United States is caught with its pants down as pedophile priests are exposed.

1999   Bishop John Shelby Spong proves he is one of us when he publishes *The Sin of Scriptures*.

2001   Sam Harris receives undivine inspiration to write *The End of Faith*.

2004   George Carlin, the world's funniest atheist, shows his unkosher side when he pens *When Will Jesus Bring the Pork Chops?*

2004   Even though some Christians claim that God is not a Democrat or a Republican, the Religious Right anoints George W. Bush as God's choice to

lead the United States, hereafter known as
the Promised Land.

2004   Mel Gibson mass markets *The Passion of the Christ*,
        thus demonstrating the marketability of religious
        violence.

2006   Daniel Dennett's, Sam Harris's, and Richard
        Dawkins's books hit the best-seller lists posing the
        question, "Is America Atheistic?"

2007   Rep. Peter Stark (D-CA) touts himself as the first
        known atheist in Congress. Praise be to Science!

2665   Atheist elected president of the United States.

2666   Hell freezes over.

APPENDIX B

INTERVIEW WITH HEMANT, AKA THE FRIENDLY ATHEIST

Following is a conversation with Hemant Mehta, the Friendly Atheist and author of I Sold My Soul on eBay.[1]

Q: **How is a Friendly Atheist different from this crop of New Atheists?**

Hemant: A Friendly Atheist, in my experience, has more in common with the bulk of atheists we all know. We don't hate religion. We want our beliefs respected, and we know that the only way to ever convince others that supernatural beliefs are not worth holding is to engage with them in positive dialogue. The New Atheists seem to turn off those they need to reach the most!

Q: **Why do you feel Dawkins, Harris, and Dennett are so popular these days?**

Hemant: They're tapping into a belief that many people hold, but have rarely dared to say out loud: That atheism is the most realistic reflection of life: that religion is nonsense. While I may disagree with their styles, there's no denying that these authors are coming out swinging and many nonreligious people are glad to finally have spokespeople to express what they've felt for so long.

Q: **What about their message resonates with you?**

Hemant: The idea that this life is unbelievably rare and precious. Evolution could have worked so many different ways, and yet we are here today. It's incredible. And we should all be living our lives as we see fit, without stopping others from doing the same.

Q: **Why are you not one of their disciples?**

Hemant: In message, I am. In tone and style, I'm not. I'd much rather engage in a dialogue with religious people. I know I have the facts behind me, and as an atheist, I shouldn't fear holding my own in a debate or conversation. The "New Atheists" appear as if they'd like nothing to do with anyone who proclaims a religion.

Q: **Why did you sell your soul on eBay?**

Hemant: I had never really visited any place of worship other than my own. I wanted to explore these faiths, while at the same time asking worshippers and pastors questions about why they believed what they did. eBay seemed like an interesting way to get people interested in the project. It worked for other religiously driven ideas like Virgin Mary on a grilled cheese sandwich! :)

Q: How did you interact with Off-the-Map, once they bought your soul for $504?

Hemant: We made a deal where I would go to approximately ten churches for them and write about my observations on their Web site. The critiques I offered would show Christians how they come across to an atheist like myself. As it turned out, many Christians shared my likes and dislikes.

Q: In your experience church shopping, how did churches alienate you?

Hemant: The churches that never required the worshippers to think for themselves and simply told everyone what to say or do never appealed to me. Neither did churches that encouraged prayer over action, crusaded against science, or believed that a hand on your body would cure back problems. If they ever want to reach out to people of other faiths or no faith, it won't happen by abandoning common sense, reason, and evidence.

Q: Conversely, what did churches do that worked for you?

Hemant: The best churches really made me think about my life and how I was living it. I'm not talking about moral issues, but rather, about my relationships with friends and family. These churches did not use sermons as a political message board. The pastors here were more concerned about fixing problems in their community than forcing everyone to believe what they did.

Q: **Why do you genuinely enjoy watching Joel Osteen?**

Hemant: I believe he epitomizes the belief that we can all do better in various areas of our lives. No one ever attacked him for being too controversial—anyone can watch him and see a genuinely nice guy making thousands of people happier each week. If more people followed his vision of Christianity, we'd all be better off. It doesn't mean I agree with his interpretations of the Bible or his reasoning that everything good in life is a gift from God. I don't. However, this is religion that isn't hurting other people, and for that, I'd commend him.

Q: **If you were to return to church, which church(es) that you visited would you go back to again, and why?**

Hemant: Some of the megachurches were very appealing during the sermon—places like Willow Creek or Lakewood—however programs they held outside the weekend sermons were quite disturbing, like when they bring in a speaker endorsing intelligent design without bringing in a credible evolutionary biologist. I was also impressed by Via Christus, a house church I saw—the people here were as fed up with the hypocritical pastors and moneymaking churches as many atheists. They worshipped in their own way and built a small, close-knit community of their own, and I liked that, even though I didn't share their faith.

Q: What could Christians do to improve their public persona?

Hemant: Christians could focus more on helping fix problems in their communities rather than focusing on converting everyone they meet. They could work together with people of other faiths or no faith. They talk about helping the world, but so few churches actually do it. I know proselytizing is a duty that many evangelicals feel they must do, but by abandoning that belief, and having their actions speak for them, they'd end up changing a lot of minds about what Christianity is all about. The fact that this doesn't happen often is, in fact, why some atheists lose their faith. We see the good Christianity can do, but it requires cherry-picking from the Bible. Many Christians are afraid to do this, for obvious reasons, and their inability to do so will be their ultimate downfall.

Q: What advice would you give for a Christian who wants to dialogue with agnostics, skeptics, and atheists?

Hemant: Christians have to understand why atheists believe what we do. Read the books by the "New Atheists,"

Appendix B

ignore the harsh rhetoric for a bit, and look at the reasons they give for not believing in God. If that's too much to do, just ask us questions. We're more than willing to talk. And please do not think that there is some magical Bible verse that will change our minds.

Q: **Setting aside church—what's your reaction to Jesus of Nazareth's ministry and teachings?**

Hemant: I've heard some good things and bad things about Jesus. He wasn't perfect. No one is. But if we can learn a lesson from the good things he might have done in his life, maybe we can understand that talking to people we may not agree with is a virtue.

NOTES

PREFACE

1. "God Debate: Sam Harris vs. Rick Warren," *Newsweek*, April 9, 2007, http://www.msnbc.msn.com/id/17889148/site/newsweek/page/1. All rights reserved. Used by permission and protected by the Copyright Laws of the United States. The printing, copying, redistribution, or retransmission of the Material without express written permission is prohibited.

2. Mike Yaconelli, as quoted on Youth Specialties Web site's "Reflections on Mike Yaconelli," http://www.youthspecialties.com/yaconelli/words/wordsfrommike.php.

3. "Satire," By permission. From the *Merriam-Webster Online Dictionary* © 2007 by Merriam-Webster Inc. (www.Merriam-Webster.com).

4. Robert Darden, personal e-mail, June 20, 2007.

5. For those desiring an in-depth romp of satire throughout the ages, check out *The Dictionary of the History of Ideas*, http://etext.virginia.edu/cgi-local/DHI/dhi.cgi?id=dv4-29 (accessed June 20, 2007).

INTRODUCTION

1. Brian McLaren, "On Atheism," On Faith–*Washington Post*, December 27, 2006, http://newsweek.washingtonpost.com/onfaith/brian_d_mclaren/2006/12/on_atheism.html.

2. See James Wood, "The Celestial Teapot," *The New Republic*, December 18, 2006, http://www.tnr.com/doc.mhtml?i=20061218&s=wood121806.

3. "Americans Struggle with Religion's Role at Home and Abroad," Pew Research Center for the People & The Press Web site, March 20, 2002, http://people-press.org/reports/print.php3?ReportID=150.

4. Becky Garrison, *Rising from the Ashes: Rethinking Church* (New York: Seabury Books, 2007).

5. Becky Garrison, "Christian vs. Atheist Celebrity Death Match," God's Politics blog, May 7, 2007, http://blog.beliefnet.com/godspolitics/2007/05. This article appeared originally on www.beliefnet.com, the leading website for faith, spirituality, inspiration & more. Used with permission. All rights reserved.

6. For an illuminating insight profiling the origins of the term "Brights," see Gary Wolf, "The Church of the Non-Believers," *Wired*, November 2006, http://www.wired.com/wired/archive/14.11/atheism.html.

7. "The New Atheism," *Front Toward Enemy*, http://fronttowardenemy.wordpress.com/2006/10/27/the-new-atheism.

8. Alister McGrath, *The Twilight of Atheism: The Rise and Fall of Disbelief in the Modern World* (New York: Ebury, 2004), 46. Reprinted by permission of The Random House Group Ltd.

9. Ibid., 1.

10. My quick romp through McGrath's research can barely do justice to his work. Those desiring an in-depth critique of my short snapshots would be wise to read *The Twilight of Atheism* in its entirety, as well as McGrath and Joanna Collicut McGrath, *The Dawkins Delusion: Atheist Fundamentalism and the Denial of the Divine* (Downers Grove, IL: InterVarsity Press, 2007).

11. McGrath, *The Twilight of Atheism*, 25.

12. For an eye-opening documentary into the life and times of Tammy Faye Bakker Messing, check out *The Eyes of Tammy Faye*, http://www.eyesoftammyfaye.com; Jan Crouch's hair can be seen at TBN—*Trinity Broadcasting Network* Web site, http://www.tbn.org.

13. Voltaire as quoted in McGrath, *The Twilight of Atheism*, 25.

14. McGrath, 27.

15. See Matt Bean, "Seeing the Future—or Just Dollar Signs?" *Court TV*, January 17, 2002, http://www.courttv.com/news/feature/cleo/misscleo_ctv.html.

16. For further information on this ungodly scholar, check out the Friedrich Nietzsche Society at http://www.fns.org.uk.

17. Star Wars Databank, http://www.starwars.com/databank/organization/stormtroopers.

18. See Richard W. Fox, *Jesus in America* (San Francisco: HarperSanFrancisco, 2004) for a historical overview of how Jesus has been depicted throughout American history.

19. John D. Caputo, *Philosophy and Theology* (Nashville, TN: Abingdon Press, 2006), 35.

20. McGrath, *Twilight of Atheism*, 219.

21. "The Humanist Interview with Greg Epstein, Humanist Chaplain of Harvard," the Secularist Student Alliance Web site, http://www.secularstudents.org/node/602.

22. Ann Coulter's infamous comment, "We should invade their countries, kill their leaders and convert them to Christianity," was posted on AnnCoulter.com, September 12, 2001, http://www.anncoulter.org/columns/2001/091301.htm.

23. Diganta, "The Atheism FAQ with Richard Dawkins," Desicritics.org, http://desicritics.org/2007/05/26/003610.php.

24. Dawkins, "Are We Better Off Without Religion?: The Intelligence2 Debate," *Times Online*, March 29, 200, http://www.timesonline.co.uk/tol/news/. Search by article title.

25. Richard Dawkins, "How Dare You Call Me a Fundamentalist," *Times*, May 12, 2007, http://www.timesonline.co.uk/tol/news/. Search by article title.

26. Andrew Brown, "Dawkins the Dogmatist" first appeared in the October 2006 issue of *Prospect* magazine (www.prospect-magazine.co.uk).

27. *Animal House*, Universal Pictures (1978).

28. Jack Miles, "Book Review: 'God Is Not Great: How Religion Poisons Everything,' by Christopher Hitchens," *Los Angeles Times*, April 29, 2007.

29. Marshall McLuhan as quoted in McGrath, *The Twilight of Atheism*, 273.

30. I reference the New Atheists using masculine nouns because, while I know that atheists encompass the full range of humanity, so far I haven't seen the female equivalent of Dawkins, Harris, and Dennett. Not saying that's a bad thing, mind you.

31. See Charles Moore, "Militant Atheists: Too Clever for Their Own Good," *London Telegraph*, April 7, 2007, http://www.telegraph.co.uk/opinion/main.jhtml?xml=/opinion/2007/04/07/do0701.xml.

32. Ibid.

33. Yale Divinity School Web site, http://www.yale.edu/divinity.

34. Terry Eagleton, "Lunging, Flailing, Mispunching," *London Review of Books*, October 19, 2006, http://www.lrb.co.uk/v28/n20/eagl01_.html.

35. H. Allen Orr, "A Mission to Convert," *New York Review of Books* 54, no. 1, January 11, 2007, http://www.nybooks.com/articles/19775.

NOTES

36. Ibid.
37. Exerpts from *The God Delusion* by Richard Dawkins. Copyright © 2006 by Richard Dawkins. Reprinted by permission of Houghton Mifflin Company. All rights reserved.
38. See Rob Bell, *Velvet Elvis: Repainting the Christian Faith* (Grand Rapids, MI: Zondervan, New Ed edition, 2006); "Tom Cruise Is Nuts," http://www.tomcruiseisnuts.com; the Worldwide Forgiveness Alliance Web site, http://www.forgivenessday.org; the World Subud Association Web site, http://www.subud.org; and the Kabbalah Center Web site, http://www.kabbalah.com.
39. Daniel C. Dennett, "The God Delusion," *The New York Review of Books,* March 1, 2007, http://www.nybooks.com/articles/19928.
40. David Marshall, *The Truth Behind the New Atheism* (Eugene, OR: Harvest House Publishers, 2007), 92.
41. See American Idol: Official Fox Site, www.americanidol.com.
42. See The Wizard of Oz on DVD – The Official Site, http://thewizardofoz.warnerbros.com; for those of you not immersed in the Christian subculture, WWJD stands for "What Would Jesus Do?" It's a saying popularized in the 1990s and emblazoned on bracelets, T-shirts, bumper stickers, and probably just about any object where some marketing guru could get this saying to stick in order to make a Bible buck.
43. See the National Council of Churches USA Web site for a full-blown interdenominational display of material guaranteed to cure spiritual cravings, http://www.ncccusa.org.
44. Those needing a seventies-inspired nostalgia fix can log on to "I Love the 70s" at TV.com, http://www.tv.com/i-love-the-70s/show/21163/summary.html.
45. "The Three Wise Monkeys," *Newsfinder,* http://www.newsfinder.org/site/more/the_three_wise_monkeys.
46. Andrew Higgins, "As Religious Strife Grows, Europe's Atheists Seize Pulpit," *Wall Street Journal,* April 12, 2007, http://pewforum.org/news/display.php?NewsID=13213.
47. "Larry Charles Doc Piques Biz," Variety Fest Central Web site, February 8, 2007, http://weblogs.variety.com/fest_central/2007/02/larry_charles_d.html.

Notes

Hitchens Forfeits Fight

1. Hatchette Book Group USA, personal letter, June 6, 2007.
2. "Warner Twelve: Mission Statement," *Publishers Weekly*, July 21, 2005, http://www.publishersweekly.com/article/CA628327.html.
3. William Occam came up with the principle of parsimony, aka "Occam's razor." This principle declares that "theories should not be any more complex than necessary." Or, as Occam put it metaphysically, theories should not "multiply entities unnecessarily." Suppose Isaac Newton had watched the apple fall and exclaimed, "I've got it! Apples are being caught in a tug-of-war between gremlins pulling them up and trolls pulling them down, and trolls are stronger!" Occam would have retorted, "Okay, Isaac, your theory does account for all the observable facts, but get with the program—keep it simple!" Thomas Cathcart and Daniel Klein, *Plato and a Platypus Walk into a Bar . . . Understanding Philosophy Through Jokes* (New York: Adams Image, 2007), 24.
4. William Shakespeare, *Macbeth*, Act 5, Scene 5.

Going Gonzo Against God

1. Francis Collins, *The Language of God* (New York: Free Press, 2006), 162. Reprinted with the permission of Simon & Schuster Adult Publishing Group. All rights reserved.
2. Joan Roughgarden, *Evolution and Christian Faith* (Washington, DC: Island Press, 2006), 10.
3. Tony Campolo, *Letters to a Young Evangelical* (New York: Basic Books, 2007), 239–40.
4. See the Official Peanuts Website: Meet the Gang – Linus, http://www.snoopy.com/comics/peanuts/meet_the_gang/meet_linus.html.
5. Becky Garrison, "Beavis and Butthead Are Saved," *The Wittenburg Door*, May/June 1994.
6. See Becky Garrison, "Jesus Died for THIS?: A Reflection Of Jesus's Ministry Juxtaposed Against Our Contemporary Political Landscape," *The Ooze*, November 7, 2005, http://www.theooze.com/articles/article.cfm?id=1461.
7. See Dr. Seuss, *Horton Hears a Who* (New York: Random House Books for Young Readers, 1954).

NOTES

8. See John Chapman, *Know and Tell the Gospel* (London: Hodder & Stoughton General Division, 1976).

9. "Profile: Colin Powell," *BBC News*, November 15, 2004, http://news.bbc.co.uk/1/hi/world/americas/2246150.stm.

10. Available at the White House Web site, http://www.whitehouse.gov/infocus/iraq/iraq_strategy_nov2005.html.

11. For a full description of the New Atheist demands, see Sam Harris, "An Atheist Manifesto," TruthDig.com, December 7, 2005, http://www.truthdig.com/dig/item/200512_an_atheist_manifesto/.

12. Jon Meacham, "Is God Real? The Debate over Religion," *Newsweek*, April 9, 2007, http://www.msnbc.msn.com/id/17889147/site/newsweek. All rights reserved. Used by permission and protected by the Copyright Laws of the United States. The printing, copying, redistribution, or retransmission of the Material without express written permission is prohibited.

13. Keith Ward, *Is Religion Dangerous?* (Grand Rapids, MI: William B. Eerdmans Publishing Company, 2006), 74.

14. Gary Wolfe, "Church of the Non-Believers." *Wired* [This is the first citation of this source. What is it?]

15. "The New Atheism/Anti-Religion Movement," *Modern Humanist*, November 13, 2006, http://www.modernhumanist.com/?p=46.

16. See Garrison, "Coulter Christianity?," God's Politics blog, March 7, 2007, http://blog.beliefnet.com/godspolitics/2007/03/becky-garrison-coulter-christianity.html. This article appeared originally on www.beliefnet.com, the leading website for faith, spirituality, inspiration & more. Used with permission. All rights reserved.

17. Wood, "The Celestial Teapot."

18. Wolfe, "Church of the Non-Believers."

19. For a comprehensive list of patriot and neo-Nazi groups, see the Southern Poverty Law Center Web site, http://www.splcenter.org/index.jsp.

20. Dave Silverman, personal email (February 24, 2007).

21. Orr, "A Mission to Convert."

22. Sam Schulman, "Without God, Gall Is Permitted," *Wall Street Journal*, January 5, 2007, http://www.opinionjournal.com/taste/?id=110009482.

23. Ibid.

24. Alvin Plantinga, "The Dawkins Confusion," *Books & Culture*, March/April 2007, http://www.christianitytoday.com/bc/2007/002/1.21.html.

25. Given that RJ Reynolds Tobacco Company funded much of Wake Forest University during my tenure (1979–83), they clearly didn't have a problem with smoking per se. You just had to stick to cancer sticks.

26. See Bertrand Russell, "Is There a God," *The Collected Papers of Bertrand Russell*, Volume 11: Last Philosophical Testament, 194369, ed. John C. Slater and Peter Kollner, (London: Routledge, 1997), 543–48.

27. The term "Pastafarian" is a combination of words *pasta* and *Rastafarian*. For more information about this parody, check out "Open Letter to Kansas School Board," at the Church of the Flying Spaghetti Monster Web site, http://www.vengaza.org/about/open-letter.

28. Wood, "Celestial Teapot."

29. For a more in-depth analysis of Pat Robertson's hypocrisy, see Becky Garrison, *Red and Blue God, Black and Blue Church*, (San Francisco: Jossey Bass, 2006), 3–5.

30. Eagleton, "Lunging, Flailing, Mispunching,"

31. Excerpts from *The God Delusion* by Richard Dawkins. Copyright © 2006 by Richard Dawkins. Reprinted by permission of Houghton Mifflin Company. All rights reserved.

32. See Becky Garrison, *Contemplating Coulter Christianity* (Amazon.com Short, 2006). Search at Amazon.com by work's title.

33. Nick West, "An Imaginary Deity Is Denounced and Debunked," *Tribune Book Reviews*, http://richarddawkins.net/article,456,An-imaginary-deity-is-denounced-and-debunked,Nick-West-Tribune-book-reviews.

34. Dawkins, *The God Delusion*, 92. See also Flavius Josephus, *Antiquities of the Jews*, 18.3.3.3, http://www.ccel.org/j/josephus/works/ant-18.htm.

35. See Matthew 28:18–19 and Luke 24:46–49 for starters.

36. Sam Harris, *The End of Faith: Religion, Terror and the Future of Reason* (New York: W. W. Norton, 2004), 65.

37. Laura Sheahen, "Why Religion Must End: Interview with Sam Harris," Beliefnet.com, http://www.beliefnet.com/story/191/story_19107_1.html. This article appeared originally on www.beliefnet.com, the leading website for faith, spirituality, inspiration & more. Used with permission. All rights reserved.

38. See the "American Academy of Religion Online Program Book" at the American Academy of Religion Web site: http://www.aarweb.org.

39. http://www.ufocongress.com.

40. Dawkins, *God Delusion*, 237. Those who use colored golf balls to test the validity of Scripture, worship the goddess Sophia through milk 'n' honey Eucharists, and other *Door*-worthy shenanigans should be viewed as colorful albeit clueless clowns, not serious scholars. Note: Here I admit I can't be completely unbiased toward Bishop John Shelby Spong. When I was at Yale Divinity School, he lived on my dorm room floor for a month during the spring of 1989. So, I was subjected to daily sightings of a grown bishop walking to the communal bathroom in his purple slippers that his mommy knit for him, and, of course, a purple bathrobe. Also, I remember hearing him holding court during meals and coffee hours with his fawning sycophants gathered at his feet like devout doggies. Those seekers like myself, who dared to dialogue and differ with JSS, were dismissed with a scornful sneer. So I can't take the guy seriously one whit, though I must confess that encounters like this one inspired me to become a religious satirist.

41. John Shelby Spong, *Why Christianity Must Change or Die* (San Francisco: HarperSanFrancisco, 1999) from an excerpt posted at Harper Collins Australia Web site, http://www.harpercollins.com.au/global_scripts/product_catalog/book_xml.asp?isbn=0060675365&tc=cx.

42. *The Book of Common Prayer (1979) of the Episcopal Church*, (New York: Church Publishing), 513.

43. Plantinga, "The Dawkins Confusion."

44. If the reference to Henry VIII makes no sense, then go to your European History professor and ask for your money back (this does not apply to those who snoozed instead of studied). See "Henry VIII (1509–1547)," the Official Website of the British Monarchy, http://www.royal.gov.uk /output/Page19.asp; Michael Lampen, "Bishop James Pike: Visionary or Heretic," the Grace Cathedral Web site, http://www.gracecathedral.org/enrichment/crypt/cry_20011114.shtml; and "What Makes Us Anglican," the Episcopal Church: Seekers Center Web site, http://www.episco-palchurch.org/17041_17013_ENG_HTM.htm?menu=menu16975.

45. "Atheism." By permission. From the *Merriam-Webster Online Dictionary* © 2007 by Merriam-Webster Inc. (www.Merriam-Webster.com).

46. Gordy Slack, "Dissecting God," *Salon*, February 8, 2006. This article first appeared at http://www.salon.com. An online version remains in the Salon archives. Reprinted with permission.

47. Harris, "There Is No God (and You Know It)," *The Huffington Post*, October 6, 2005, http://www.huffingtonpost.com/sam-harris/there-is-no-god-and-you-_b_8459.html.

48. John Shelby Spong, *Jesus For the Non Religious* (San Francisco: HarperSanFrancisco, 2007), 214. Reprinted by permission of HarperCollins Publishers.

49. Stephen Tomkins, *A Short History of Christianity*. (Grand Rapids, MI: Wm. B. Eerdmans Publishing, 2005), 25.

50. Spong, "Human Definitions of God Need Revision," *Washington Post*, January 1, 2007, http://newsweek.washingtonpost.com/onfaith/john_shelby_spong/2007/01/i_welcome_the_attention_that_1.html.

51. Brian Braiker. "God's Numbers," *Newsweek*, March 30, 2007, http://www.msnbc.msn.com/id/17879317/site/newsweek. All rights reserved. Used by permission and protected by the Copyright Laws of the United States. The printing, copying, redistribution, or retransmission of the Material without express written permission is prohibited.

52. See Stephen Prothero, *Religious Literacy: What Every American Needs to Know—and Doesn't* (San Francisco: HarperSanFrancisco, 2007).

53. For those wishing to engage in some postmodern prancing, check out James K.A. Smith,. *Who's Afraid of Postmodernism?: Taking Derrida, Lyotard, and Foucault to Church* (Grand Rapids: Baker Academic, 2006)

54. Here I must credit Tony Jones, National Coordinator of Emergent Village, for coining an invigorating term to describe a twenty-first-century alpha male theological debate.

55. Brian McLaren, *Everything Must Change* (Nashville: Thomas Nelson, Inc., 2007), 23.

56. C. S. Lewis, *Mere Christianity* from *The Complete C. S. Lewis Signature Classics* (San Francisco: HarperSanFrancisco, 2002), 78.

57. Ward, "Is Religion Dangerous?" 90.

DOES GOD MATTER?

1. Victor Stenger, *God: The Failed Hypothesis* (Amherst, NY: Prometheus Books, 2007), 156.

2. Ibid., 173.

3. For those wishing to delve deeper into my admittedly warped child-hood musical collection, my favorite rendition of "Plastic Jesus" to date is the Billy Idol version at http://www.ifilm.com/video/2682805. "The Vatican Rag" can be found on Tom Lehrer's *That Was the Week That Was* (Los Angeles, Reprise/WEA, 1965). The actual existence of "Wolfgang Amadeus Mozart Was a Dirty Old Man" was reported by *Time*, October 20, 1967, http://www.time.com/time/printout/0,8816,902094,00.html. Suffice to say, child psychologist and my late grandfather, Dr. Karl Claudius Garrison Sr., had a field day trashing his son's child-rearing practices. While Gramps raised many valid points, at least I developed a career as a religious satirist out of my childhood traumas.

4. Orr, "A Mission to Convert."

5. See Stenger, *God: The Failed Hypothesis*, 184–85 for a full explanation of why he thinks Jesus is a figment of the faithful's imagination.

6. See Matthew 28:1–6; Mark 16:1–6; Luke 24:1–7; and John 20:1.

7. See Luke 24:13–35.

8. See Matthew 27:66 and Mark 15:46.

9. See "The Christian History Timeline: Persecution in the Early Church," *Christian History*, July 1, 1990, http://ctlibrary.com/3732.

10. See Marshall Thompson, "Scholars Criticize New Jesus Documentary," February 26, 2007, http://www.wset.com/news/stories/0207/400767.html.

11. See Matthew 27:38, Mark 15:27, and Luke 23:32–43.

12. See John 18:36.

13. Lewis, *Mere Christianity*, 30.

14. For a full-blown account of Dawkins's meme madness, pick up his *The Selfish Gene* (New York: Oxford University Press, 1976).

15. Lewis Wolpert, *Six Impossible Things Before Breakfast: The Evolutionary Origins of Belief* (New York: W. W. Norton), 30.

16. Orr, "A Mission to Convert."

17. See Irene R. Prusher, "A Theme Park for the Holy Land? *Christian Science Monitor*, http://www.csmonitor.com/2005/1110/p06s01-wome.htm; and The Holy Land Experience Web site, http://www.theholylandexperience.com.

NOTES

18. Dennett, *Darwin's Dangerous Idea: Evolution and the Meanings of Life* (New York: Simon & Schuster Adult Publishing Group, 1995), 515. Reprinted with permission.

19. See Peter Rollins, *How (Not) to Speak of God* (Orleans, MA: Paraclete Press, 2006). Used by permission of Paraclete Press, www.paracletepress.com. For those desiring a quickie intro into St. Anselm's proofs for the existence of God, check out "The Real New Atheism" at Rollins's *Ignite* blog, January 17, 2007, http://www.ignite.cd/blogs/Pete/index.cfm?postid=610.

20. See "John Locke," *Stamford Encyclopedia of Philosophy*, http://plato.stanford.edu/entries/locke.

21. The National Academy of Sciences Web site, http://www.nasonline.org/site/PageServer.

22. *Teaching About Evolution and the Nature of Science* (Washington, DC: National Academies Press, 1998), 58. Available at http://books.nap.edu/openbook/0309063647/html/58.html.

23. See David Van Biema, "God vs. Science," *Time*, November 05, 2006, http://www.time.com/time/magazine/article/0,9171,1555132,00.html.

24. Stenger, *God: The Failed Hypothesis*, 85; Even though I am quoting only Stenger, I am using the pronoun "their" to denote that at least Dawkins and Harris must share Stenger's beliefs. After all, they did endorse his book.

25. Fox, *Jesus in America*, 406. Reprinted by permission of HarperCollins Publishers.

26. I can trace my lineage back twelve generations through Roger Williams's son, Joseph, and back thirteen generations through his son, Daniel. Makes sense that the inbred descendent of a rebellious Anglican clergyman would become a religious satirist. But I digress.

27. Subscribe to the *Wittenburg Door*'s "Insider Newsletter" (www.wittenburgdoor.com) to keep up with the various odd and sundry Christian capers.

28. Collins, *The Language of God*, 40.

29. Moore, "Militant Atheists."

30. Peter Rollins, "Christianity and Truth," *Ignite* blog, April 15, 2007, http://www.ignite.cd/blogs/Pete/index.cfm?postid=718.

31. Edward T. Oakes, "Reason and Pop Atheism," *First Things*, Monday, January 22, 2007, http://www.firstthings.com/onthesquare/?p=599.

ALL FAITHFUL AREN'T FOOLS

1. Sam Harris, "Author Q&A for *Letter to a Christian Nation*" as posted on Random House's Web site, http://www.randomhouse.com/catalog/display.pperl?isbn=9780307265777&view=auqa.

2. Stephen Tomkins, "1 1/2 Cheers for Richard Dawkins," http://ship-of-fools.com/Features/2006/dawkins.html.

3. "Joe Bob's America," *The Joe Bob Report*, http://www.joebobbriggs.com.

4. See Roger Corman: The Official DVD Website, http://video.movies.go.com/rogercorman/index.html.

5. Dawkins, *The God Delusion*, 310–15.

6. For additional information on John Waters, see the Welcome to Dreamland Web site, http://www.dreamlandnews.com.

7. "Monty Python's Flying Circus," BBC, September 22, 1970 Show #60440, http://www.tv.com/monty-python-s-flying-circus/show/3412/episode_guide.html.

8. Matt. 24:14 NKJV.

9. "Statement by Charles Taylor at the Templeton Prize Conference," March 14, 2007, http://www.templetonprize.org/ct_statement.html.

10. William Wilberforce, rev. and updated by Bob Beltz, *Real Christianity* (Ventura, CA: Regal Books, 2006), 45.

11. Evangelicals for Darfur Web site, http://go.sojo.net/campaign/evangelicalsfordarfur.

12. Luke 18:16–17 NKJV.

13. "Facts on Children," UNICEF Web site, http://www.unicef.org/media/9475.html.

14. See Matthew 14:13–21, Mark 6:34–44, Luke 9:10–17, John 6:1–14.

15. Dawkins, *The God Delusion*, 319.

16. Ibid., 320.

17. "What Is the Hell House Outreach?" New Destiny Christian Center Web site, http://www.godestiny.org/hell_house/HH_kitWhat.cfm.

18. "The New Intolerance," *Christianity Today*, January 25, 2007, http://www.christianitytoday.com/40585.

19. Tom Gilson, "Child's Play from Dawkins: Religion Isn't Bad for Kids," *The Daily Press* (Newport News, VA), February 14, 2007, reprinted in *Breakpoint*, February 28, 2007, http://www.breakpoint.org/listingarticle.asp?ID=6192.

20. See Ed Lavandera, "Dodge City Showdown at Funeral," March 7, 2006, http://www.cnn.com/2006/US/03/06/btsc.lavandrera.funerals/index.html.

21. See *Paranoia: The Conspiracy & Paranormal Reader*, http://www.paranoiamagazine.com.

22. See the Westboro Baptist Church Home Page, http://www.godhatesfags.com/main/index.html. Pat Robertson's 9/11 remarks were reprinted in "You Helped This Happen," September 13, 2007, http://www.beliefnet.com/story/87/story_8770_1.html. This article appeared originally on www.beliefnet.com, the leading website for faith, spirituality, inspiration & more. Used with permission. All rights reserved. See also Ann Coulter as quoted by UPI International, http://www.upi.com/NewsTrack/Quirks/Ann_Coulter_calls_John_Edwards_faggot/20070302-105935-6328r/. Also see Garrison, "Coulter Christianity?" Note: I was penning this chapter right as Ann Coulter made this crack. All I had to do was substitute Democratic presidential candidate John Edwards instead of former vice president Al Gore, former president Bill Clinton or Senator Hillary Clinton. This political pundit has a long history of questioning the sexuality of Democrats while giving Republicans like Mark Foley a free ride. See Becky Garrison, "What to Do About Haggard," *The Ooze*, December 7, 2006, http://www.theooze.com/articles/article.cfm?id=1573, for an in-depth look at Coulter & Company's partisan take on sex and politics.

23. A very practical book I found to be invaluable in this lifelong quest has been Marcia Ford, *The Sacred Art of Forgiveness: Forgiving Ourselves and Others Through God's Grace* (Woodstock, VT: Skylight Paths Publishing, 2006).

24. Nora Gallagher, "Cutting at Christianity." *Los Angeles Times.* March 24, 2006, http://www.noragallagher.org/html/article2.html.

25. www.thesimpleway.org.

26. Matt. 22:37–40 NKJV.

27. My suggested reading material for someone wishing to explore these men's writings would be: Dietrich Bonhoeffer, *The Cost of Discipleship* (London: SCM Press; New Ed edition, 2001); Martin Luther King Jr., *A*

Testament of Hope: The Essential Writings and Speeches of Martin Luther King, Jr., ed. James Washington (San Francisco: HarperSanFrancisco, 1990); and Mahatma Gandhi, *The Words of Gandhi*, ed. Richard Attenborough (New York: Newmarket Press, 2nd ed., 2001).

28. John Green and Steven Waldman, "The Twelve Tribes of American Politics," http://www.beliefnet.com/story/153/story_15355_1.html. This article appeared originally on www.beliefnet.com, the leading website for faith, spirituality, inspiration & more. Used with permission. All rights reserved.

29. See Romans 12:4–5.

30. Sam Harris, "Bombing Our Illusions," *Huffington Post*, October 10, 2005, http://www.huffingtonpost.com/sam-harris/bombing-our-illusions_b_8615.html.

31. Harris, *The End of Faith*, 15.

32. Benjamin Shobert, "If Dawkins Makes Sense to Me, Does That Make Me an Atheist?," *SOMA Review*, January 20, 2007, http://www.somareview.com/ifdawkinsmakessense.cfm (as accessed on March 2, 2007).

33. Sheahen, "Why Religion Must End."

34. Miroslav Volf, personal e-mail, August 22, 2007.

35. Eagleton, "Lunging, Flailing, Mispunching."

36. See Daniel Dennett, *Breaking the Spell: Religion as a Natural Phenomenon* (New York: Viking, 2006), 300.

37. Andrew Jones, "The Skinny on New Atheism," TallSkinnyKiwi blog, December 08, 2006, http://www.tallskinnykiwi.typepad.com/tallskinnykiwi/2006/12/the_skinny_on_n.html.

38. See David Segal, "Atheist Evangelist: In His Bully Pulpit, Sam Harris Devoutly Believes That Religion Is the Root of All Evil," *Washington Post*, October 26, 2006, C01, http://www.washingtonpost.com/wp-dyn/content/article/2006/10/25/AR2006102501998.html.

39. Richard Dawkins, "Time to Stand Up," September 2001, http://ffrf.org/timely/dawkins.php.

40. Those desiring a more in-depth critique of the interfaith community's post-9/11 responses (or the lack thereof) can check out Garrison, *Red and Blue God, Black and Blue Church*, "Chapter 2, Guns God 'n' Ground Zero," 11–28.

41. Ibid., 25.

42. http://www.where-to-turn.org.

43. Shane Claiborne, *Irresistible Revolution* (Grand Rapids: Zondervan, 2006), 159.

44. Sam Harris, interview by Stephen Colbert, *The Colbert Report*, April 25, 2006.

45. Marcus Borg, "What Is the Significance of the Cross and the Crucifixion of Jesus?," http://www.explorefaith.org/questions/cross.html.

46. Henri Nouwen, *Behold the Beauty of the Lord* (Notre Dame, IN: Ave Maria Press, 1987), 19–20.

THE WRATH OF SAM HARRIS TAKES ON THE COMPASSIONATE CHRIST: GET READY TO RUMBLE!

1. Bethany Saltman, "The Temple of Reason: Sam Harris on Why Religion Puts the World at Risk," *The Sun*, http://www.thesunmagazine.org/369_Harris.pdf.

2. "Americans Struggle with Religion's Role at Home and Abroad."

3. Braiker, "God's Numbers."

4. Nigel Spivey, "Are We Better Off Without Religion?: The Intelligence2 Debate."

5. "Why Are Atheists So Angry?," *Jewcy*, November 16, 2006, http://www.jewcy.com/dialogue/monday_why_are_atheists_so_angry_sam_harris.

6. Dennis Prager, "Why Are Atheists So Angry? God Is No "Useful Delusion, Day 4," *Jewcy*, November 21, 2006, http://www.jewcy.com/dialogue/11-21/day_4_prager_why_are_atheists_so_angry.

7. This comparison was also made by Segal in "Atheist Evangelist."

8. See Sam Harris and Andrew Sullivan, "Is Religion 'Built upon Lies'?" Belief.net, http://www.beliefnet.com/story/209/story_20904_1.html. This article appeared originally on www.beliefnet.com, the leading website for faith, spirituality, inspiration & more. Used with permission. All rights reserved.

9. McLaren, "On Atheism."

10. Ibid.

11. Matt. 5:13 NKJV.

12. I cannot do justice to centuries of scholarship debating the concept of free will. I bring this subject up because the New Atheists keep insisting that Christians seem to think that God is totally responsible for man's actions, a concept that goes against orthodox Christian teachings. For those who would like to delve into this topic further, I suggest starting with C. S. Lewis's *Mere Christianity*.

13. See Genesis 4:3–8.

14. "Religion.". By permission. From the *Merriam-Webster Online Dictionary* © 2007 by Merriam-Webster Inc. (www.Merriam-Webster.com).

15. Saltman, "The Temple of Reason."

16. "Statement by Charles Taylor at the Templeton Prize Conference."

17. Reza Aslan as quoted in "Atheist Evangelist."

18. I am focusing on the Christian response to these New Atheists, as I can really only speak to the depths of my own religious tradition. I encourage those who would like to study more about the history of Islam to pick up Reza Aslan's book *No God but God: The Origins, History and Future of Islam.* (New York: Random House, reprint edition, 2006).

19. Bill Maher as quoted by Cathleen Falsani, "What They Said About God in '04," *Chicago Sun-Times*, December 31, 2004. See also http://falsani.blogspot.com/2004_12_01_archive.html.

20. David Kuo, "Jesus and Bill Maher," Beliefnet: J-Walking Web site, October 21, 2006, http://blog.beliefnet.com/jwalking/2006/10/jesus-and-bill-maher.html. This article appeared originally on www.beliefnet.com, the leading website for faith, spirituality, inspiration & more. Used with permission. All rights reserved.

21. Maher, "New Rules," *Real Time with Bill Maher*, http://www.hbo.com/billmaher/new_rules/20060331.html.

22. See Genesis 49:10, Numbers 24:17, 2 Samuel 7:12–16; Isaiah 9:6–7; Jeremiah 23:5–6; and Daniel 9:25–26 for some of the Old Testament messianic prophecies.

23. See Matthew 21:7–11 and John 12:12–15.

24. Steve Chalke, interview by Becky Garrison, *The Wittenburg Door*, January/February 2006.

25. Ibid.

26. Ibid. See John 2:13–22.

27. See the Association for Christian Retail Web site at http://www.cbaonline.org for more information on what believers can buy.

28. See Matthew 6:33. For an in-depth look at the application of the kingdom-of-God sayings in Scripture to the Christian life, check out McLaren's insightful tome, *The Secret Message of Jesus* (Nashville: Thomas Nelson, 2006).

29. Brian McLaren, interview by Becky Garrison, *The Wittenburg Door*, July/August 2007.

30. Shane Claiborne, interview by Becky Garrison, *The Wittenburg Door*, May/June 2007.

31. Matt. 5:39 NKJV.

32. Walter Wink, "Can Love Save the World," *Yes Magazine*, Winter 2002, http://www.yesmagazine.org/article.asp?ID=485.

33. Henri Nouwen, *Reaching Out* (New York: Doubleday, 1966), 73.

34. Miroslav Volf, interview by Becky Garrison, *The Wittenburg Door*, January/February 1999; For those who aren't familiar with Dr. Volf's work, this Croat-Serbian theologian embodies a theology grounded in his experiences growing up as a Christian in war-torn former Yugoslavia. So he speaks from the heart and the head, a combo I wish more theologians would follow.

35. Ibid.

36. Desmond Tutu, *No Future Without Forgiveness*. (New York: Doubleday, 1999), 265. Reprinted by permission of The Random House Group Ltd.

37. N. T. Wright, *Evil and the Justice of God* (Downers Grove, IL: InterVarsity Press, 2006), 134

38. Ibid.

39. Gareth Higgins, interview by Becky Garrison, September 6, 2007.

WHY HAVE YOU FORSAKEN ME?

1. Dawkins, *The God Delusion*, 50.

2. Nicholas D. Kristoff, "A Modest Proposal for a Truce on Religion," *New York Times*, December 3, 2006, as posted on http://www.samharris.org/site/full_text/a-modest-proposal-for-a-truce-on-religion. ©2006 by The New York Times Co. Reprinted with permission.

3. http://www.whydoesgodhateamputees.com.

4. Kristoff, "A Modest Proposal."

5. To order *The Many Faces of Benny Hinn, Version 3.0* – DVD Set, go to http://www.wittenburgdoor.com/Merchant2/merchant.mvc?Screen= PROD&Product_Code=HINN_V3&Category_Code=VID.

6. *The Book of Common Prayer (1979) of the Episcopal Church*, 358.

7. Rollins, "Revelation Verses Concealment: Barriers to Reconciliation," *Ignite* blog, April 3, 2005, http://www.ignite.cd/blogs/Pete/index.cfm?m=4&y=2005.

8. Ibid.

9. Raymond E. Brown, *Introduction to the New Testament* (New York: Doubleday, 1996), 132.

10. Rollins, "Revelation Verses Concealment."

11. Robert Darden, *Reluctant Prophets and Clueless Disciples* (Nashville, TN: Abingdon, 2006).

12. Robert Darden, interview by Mary Darden, *The Wittenburg Door*, July/August 2006.

13. James Martin, SJ, interview by Becky Garrison, *The Wittenburg Door*, September/October 2002.

14. Matt. 27:46, Mark 15:34 NKJV.

15. Stanley Hauerwas, interview by Laura Sheahen, "Why Have You Forsaken Me?," Beliefnet.com, http://www.beliefnet.com/story/161/story_16134_1.html. This article appeared originally on www.beliefnet.com, the leading website for faith, spirituality, inspiration & more. Used with permission. All rights reserved.

16. The first piece I ever wrote was an anti-Nixon one-act play, which was penned when I was nine years old. As I said, satire seemed to be my own option given my admittedly esoteric and eclectic upbringing. Now, I didn't dare call myself a writer until I sold my first piece some twenty-four years later, but a writer's soul has been there, sitting inside of me, for as long as I can remember.

17. See Becky Garrison, *Swamp Water: A Memoir* (Amazon.com Short, 2006). Search at Amazon.com by title.

18. Flannery O'Connor , ed. Sally Fitzgerald, *The Habit of Being: Letters of Flannery O'Connor* (New York: Farrar, Straus and Giroux, Reprint edition, August 1988), 100.

19. Garrison. *Swamp*.

20. Sheahen, "The Problem with God: Interview with Richard Dawkins," Beliefnet.com, http://www.beliefnet.com/story/178/story_17889.html. This article appeared originally on www.beliefnet.com, the leading website for faith, spirituality, inspiration & more. Used with permission. All rights reserved.

21. Garrison, *Swamp*.

22. I made my debut at the 1982 North Carolina Terpsichorean Ball in Raleigh, North Carolina.

23. Henri Nouwen, *Can You Drink the Cup?* (Notre Dame, IN: Ave Maria Press, 1996), 81–82.

24. Henri Nouwen, *The Wounded Healer* (New York: Doubleday Image Books, 1972).

25. St. John of the Cross, *Dark Night of the Soul*, Christian Classics Ethereal Library, http://www.ccel.org/ccel/john_cross/dark_night.html; Julian of Norwich, *Showing of Love*, http://www.umilta.net/showinglove.html; "In Memoriam: Gerald May 1940–2005," Shalem Institute for Spiritual Formation, http://www.shalem.org/gerald_may.html.

26. Bertrand Russell, *Russell on Religion* (London: Routledge, 1999), 45.

27. Martin, interview with Becky Garrison.

28. Interview with Stanley Hauerwas," http://www.sojo.net/index.cfm? action=news.display_archives&mode=current_opinion&article=CO_01 0702h.

29. Harris, "An Atheist Manifesto."

30. Deborah Caldwell, "Did God Send the Hurricane?" Beliefnet.com, http://www.beliefnet.com/story/173/story_17395_1.html. This article appeared originally on www.beliefnet.com, the leading website for faith, spirituality, inspiration & more. Used with permission. All rights reserved.

31. Campolo, *Letters to a Young Evangelical*, 96.

32. Claiborne, interview, *Wittenburg Door*.

33. These titles are among many that I consider as being "New Thought." Frederic Luskin, *Forgive for Good* (San Francisco: HarperSanFrancisco, Reprint edition, 2003); Phil McGraw, *Self Matters* (New York: Pocket Books, New Ed. edition, 2004); Marianne Williamson, *The Gift of Change* (San Francisco: HarperSanFrancisco; Reprint edition, 2006).

34. See Luke 22:1–20.

35. Matt. 18:20 NKJV.

NOTES

ONE NATION UNDER GOD?

1. Dawkins, *The God Delusion*, 45.
2. Jim Wallis, *God's Politics* (San Francisco: HarperSanFrancisco, 2004).
3. See Garrison, "Defending Roger Williams: This Time It's Personal," *The Ooze*, January 9, 2006, http://www.theooze.com/articles/article.cfm?id=1567.
4. Ibid.
5. Campolo, *Letters to a Young Evangelical*, 220.
6. Caputo, *Philosophy and Theology*, 36.
7. Google Search for "God' and 'Politics," http://www.google.com/search?hl=en&ie=ISO-8859-1&q=God+Politics&btnG=Google+Search on March 12, 2007.
8. Sam Harris, *Letter to a Christian Nation* (New York: Bantam, 2006). Reprinted by permission of The Random House Group Ltd.
9. See Paul Kengor, "Undivine Double Standard," *National Review*, http://www.nationalreview.com/comment/kengor200409070843.asp.
10. See Barrett Seaman, "Good Heavens!," *Time*, May 16, 1988, http://www.cnn.com/ALLPOLITICS/1997/05/19/back.time; "Adviser Downplays Hillary Clinton's Conversations with Eleanor Roosevelt," *CNN*, June 24, 1996, http://www.cnn.com/US/9606/24/clinton.houston; and Becky Garrison, "The Ten Commandments According to Bill Clinton," *The Wittenburg Door*, September/October 1997.
11. See Robin Martanz Henig, "Darwin's God," *New York Times Magazine*, March 4, 2007, http://www.nytimes.com/2007/03/04/magazine/04evolution.t.html.
12. Randy Kennedy, "The Grinch Delusion: An Atheist Can Believe in Christmas," *New York Times*, December 17, 2006, http://www.samharris.org/site/full_text/the-grinch-delusion-an-atheist-can-believe-in-christmas.
13. Ibid.
14. Sheahen," Why Religion Must End."
15. See the *Sojourners* Web site, http://www.sojo.net/index.cfm?action=about_us.history; Ron Sider, *Rich Christians in an Age of Hunger* (Nashville, TN: W Publishing, 1977); and *The Wittenburg Door*: Back Issues, 1971–74, http://www.wittenburgdoor.com/doorstore/backissues/71-74.html.
16. See Garrison, *Red and Blue God, Black and Blue Church*, 50–51.

17. See "Saint Clinton," http://www.saintclinton.com for further explication of former President Clinton's trademark catchphrase.

18. See the Monty Python and the Holy Grail Web site at http://www.sonypictures.com/cthe/montypython/; cf. the Monty Python's Silly Walks Generator site, http://www.sillywalksgenerator.com.

19. See the Association for Christian Retail site for Bible branding tips.

20. For an example of a truly inclusive Christian community, see Becky Garrison, "Easter for the Outcasts," God's Politics blog, March 26, 2007, http://www.beliefnet.com/blogs/godspolitics/2007/03/becky-garrison-easter-for-outcasts.html. This article appeared originally on www.beliefnet.com, the leading website for faith, spirituality, inspiration & more. Used with permission. All rights reserved.

21. Yaconelli, "Reflections."

22. Bono, *On the Move* (Nashville: Thomas Nelson, 2007), 32–33.

23. Diana Butler Bass, *Christianity for the Rest of Us* (San Francisco: HarperSanFrancisco, 2006).

24. As quoted in Becky Garrison, "Practicing the Politics of Faith," God's Politics blog, December 14, 2006, as originally posted on http://blog.beliefnet.com/godspolitics. This article appeared originally on www.beliefnet.com, the leading website for faith, spirituality, inspiration & more. Used with permission. All rights reserved.

25. Thomas Jefferson, ed. Eric Petersen, *Light and Liberty: Reflections on the Pursuit of Happiness* (New York: Random House, 2004).

I HAVE A DREAM

1. Richard Dawkins, "What Good Is Religion?" originally published in *Free Inquiry* and reprinted on Belief.net at http://www.beliefnet.com/story/75/story_7509.html. This article appeared originally on www.beliefnet.com, the leading website for faith, spirituality, inspiration & more. Used with permission. All rights reserved.

2. Play follow the money with any endowed chair or conference, and the results at times can be quite eye-opening. For example, Robert Zepps's anti–Templeton Foundation bias has to be taken into account when assessing the programming he chooses to fund. See George Johnson, "A Free-for-All on Science and Religion," *New York Times*, November 21,

2006, http://www.nytimes.com/2006/11/21/science/21belief.html?ei=
5090&en=1248e2f606e1e138&ex=1321765200&partner=
rssuserland&emc=rss&pagewanted=all.

3. For more information about the role of religion in the history of health
   care, check out "Islamic Culture and the Medical Arts: Hospitals," U.S.
   National Library of Medicine Web site, http://www.nlm.nih.gov/
   exhibition/islamic_medical/islamic_12.html; and Andrew T. Crislip,
   *From Monastery to Hospital; Christian Monasticism & the Transformation of Health
   Care in Late Antiquity.* (Ann Arbor, MI: University of Michigan Press, 2005).

4. "God Debate: Sam Harris vs. Rick Warren."

5. See "Richard Dawkins Talking to *Humanist News* in Autumn 2002,"
   British Humanist Association Web site, http://www.humanism.org.uk/
   site/cms/contentViewArticle.asp?article=1735.

6. Collins, *The Language of God*, 169.

7. Greg Easterbrook, "Does God Believe in Richard Dawkins?,"
   Beliefnet.com, http://www.beliefnet.com/story/202/story_20279.html.
   This article appeared originally on www.beliefnet.com, the leading
   website for faith, spirituality, inspiration & more. Used with permission.
   All rights reserved.

8. Ed Stetzer, "Atheism Is Back," http://theresurgence.com/
   es_blog_2006-12-08_atheism_is_back.

9. Matt. 25:35–36 NKJV.

10. See "Sitting for Justice: Woolworth's Lunch Counter," the Smithsonian
    Museum of American History Web site, http://americanhistory.si.edu/
    Brown/history/6-legacy/freedom-struggle-2.html. I know this event made
    all the Southern papers, 'cause according to family lore, the Southern
    side of my family could barely show their face at the Carolina Country
    Club following dad's brazen displays of solidarity with "the help." While
    my father never talked much about his youthful social activism, in track-
    ing down his history, I found enough anecdotal evidence to corroborate
    this story, so I am surmising that the majority of what I learned about his
    involvement with the civil rights era is reasonably accurate.

11. Steve Paulson, "The Disbeliever," *Salon.com*, July 7, 2006. Reprinted with
    permission.

12. Ibid.

13. See Matthew 5:11, 21–22, 38–41, 43–46; 10:22–23, 28; 16:24–25; 18:3,

10; 20:26–28; 22:36–40; Mark 11:25; Luke 3:14; 6:27–28; 10:26–28; 15:20–21; John 8:7; 13:34–35; 14:21, 27; 15:20–21; 16:33; 17:26; and 18:36 NKJV.

14. See "Gandhi's Source of Inspiration," the Gandhian Institution Web site, http://www.mkgandhi-sarvodaya.org/articles/inspiration.htm.

15. See "Nonviolence," Conversation at the Edge blog, January 18, 2007, http://conversationattheedge.com/2007/01/18/nonviolence/.

16. http://www.dexterkingmemorial.org.

17. See Stefan Lovgren and Tara Murphy, "Martin Luther King Jr.'s Civil Rights Dream at 40," *National Geographic News*, August 28, 2003, http://news.nationalgeographic.com/news/2003/08/0828_030828_martinlutherking.html.

18. Jean E. Barker, "Taking on Christians' Gospel Truth," *San Francisco Chronicle*, October 1, 2006, http://sfgate.com/cgi-bin/article.cgi?file=/c/a/2006/10/01/RVGFQLDQRN1.DTL.

19. "History," Human Rights Watch Web site, http://hrw.org/wr2k5/religion/4.htm.

20. "Religious Freedom," the Human Rights Watch Web site, http://hrw.org/doc/?t=religion/4.htm.

21. See Harris, "Holy Terror," *Los Angeles Times*, August 15, 2004, http://www.samharris.org/site/full_text/holy-terror; See Leviticus 25:1–55.

22. A full historical account of Jubilee 2000 can be found at the Holy See–Jubilee 2000 Web site, http://www.vatican.va/jubilee_2000/index.htm.

23. See Ron Sider, *Rich Christians in an Age of Hunger* (Nashville: Thomas Nelson, 1977), 246.

24. Ibid., 99.

25. Michael Gerson "A New Social Gospel," *Newsweek*, November 13, 2006, http://www.msnbc.msn.com/id/15566389/site/newsweek. All rights reserved. Used by permission and protected by the Copyright Laws of the United States. The printing, copying, redistribution, or retransmission of the Material without express written permission is prohibited.

26. Rick Warren in David Kuo, "Rick Warren's Second Reformation," http://www.beliefnet.com/story/177/story_17718.html. This article appeared originally on www.beliefnet.com, the leading website for faith, spirituality, inspiration & more. Used with permission. All rights reserved.

27. See their Web sites: http://www.evangelicalsforhumanrights.org;
    http://www.christiansandclimate.org; http://go.sojo.net/campaign/
    evangelicalsfordarfur.

28. Garrison, "The Christian Coalition Congressional Prayer Primer," *The
    Wittenburg Door,* May/June 1995.

Create in Me a Clean Heart

1. Dennett, *Breaking the Spell,* 83.

2. Larry McShane, "Outcry Cancels Chocolate Jesus Show," *ABC News,*
   March 31, 2007, http://abcnews.go.com/Entertainment/wireStory?id=
   2995983.

3. http://www.episcopalcursillo.org; http://www.ccci.org.

4. No, don't ask me to point out any specific praiseworthy worship leaders. I might poke fun at the more popular proponents of the slurpy spiritual stuff (see "You Go, J-O! Live from a Joel Osteen Crusade," *The
   Wittenburg Door,* March/April 2006). But there was a time when I needed
   milk before I could eat meat (see Hebrews 5:12–14). Hence, I know
   from my personal experience that one can at least get served dessert at
   these frothy events. So unless they do something particularly slimy, I'm
   liable to gently nudge these folks instead of give them a full-body
   spiritual slamming.

5. See http://jonnybaker.blogs.com and http://www.isaaceverett.com.

6. The URLs for these groups are http://www.al-anon.alateen.org and
   http://www.adultchildren.org. Note: The name for ACOA has since
   been changed to Adult Children Anonymous but I am employing the
   term that was in use during the 1980s.

7. "Adult Children Anonymous," http://www.12stepforums.net/acoa.html.

8. Harris and Sullivan, "Is Religion Built Upon Lies?"

9. "Beliefnet.com Prayer of the Day, Daily Prayer," Beliefnet.com,
   http://www.beliefnet.com/prayeroftheday/prayer_one.asp?pid=1890.
   This article appeared originally on www.beliefnet.com, the leading
   website for faith, spirituality, inspiration & more. Used with permission.
   All rights reserved.

10. "We Agnostics" in *The Big Book Online,* 4th ed. (New York: Alcoholics
    Anonymous World Services, 2001), 44–45, http://www.aa.org/
    bigbookonline/en_BigBook_chapt4.pdf.

11. See "Alcoholics Anonymous: AA at a Glance," http://www.alcoholics
   -anonymous.org/en_information_aa.cfm?PageID=10.

12. For a comprehensive listing of AA-style recovery programs, check out
   the Recovery World Web site at http://www.recovery-world.com/
   Anonymous-Recovery-Groups.html.

13. See "Alcohol Abuse and Alcoholism," *JAMA* 295, no. 17 (May 3, 2006),
   http://jama.ama-assn.org/cgi/content/full/295/17/2100.

14. "See http://www.bartleby.com/65/sc/Scientol.html and Peter
   Birkenhead, "Oprah's Ugly Secret," *Salon.com*, http://www.salon.com/
   mwt/feature/2007/03/05/the_secret/print.html.

15. See Eric Metaxas, *Amazing Grace* (San Francisco: HarperSanFrancisco,
   2007), xvi.

16. "Amazing Grace Sunday," http://www.amazinggracesunday.com.

17. Metaxas, *Amazing Grace*, 59.

18. Ibid., x.

19. Philip Yancey, forward to *John Newton: From Disgrace to Amazing Grace*, by
   Jonathan Aitken (Wheaton, IL: Crossway Books, 2007), 11.

20. Ibid., 10.

21. Acts 9:1–21.

22. See Richard Hays, *The Conversion of the Imagination: Paul as Interpreter of
   Israel's Scripture* (Grand Rapids: Wm. B. Eerdmans, 2005).

23. Dawkins, *The God Delusion*, 361.

24. Campolo, *Letters to a Young Evangelical*, 33.

25. Easterbrook, "Does God Believe in Richard Dawkins?"

26. Yaconelli, "Reflections."

27. See Basil Pennington, *Centering Prayer: Renewing an Ancient Christian Prayer
   Form*, rev. ed. (New York: Image Books, 1982).

28. See Saltman, "Temple of Reason."

29. For a modern-day take on this ancient prayer, see Dorothy Day and
   David E. Scott, *Praying in the Presence of Our Lord: With Dorothy Day*
   (Huntington, IN: Our Sunday Visitor, 2002).

30. See Saltman, "Temple of Reason."; For the full-blown mind-altering
   analysis on Harris's take on mysticism see *The End of Faith*, 221.

31. http://www.simpleliving.org; Claiborne, appendix to *Irresistible Revolution*,
   http://www.thesimpleway.org/appendix1.html.

32. Sider. *Rich Christians*, 237.

NOTES

In the Beginning . . .

1. McGrath and Collicut McGrath, *The Dawkins Delusion*, 49.
2. Garrison, *Red and Blue God, Black and Blue Church*, 83.
3. Note: I do not consider myself a card-carrying member of the Templeton Foundation fan club after they financed what can best be described as a few dubious post-9/11-related projects. However, I do appreciate their efforts to build bridges between these two disciplines.
4. For a video recap of this unbelief battle, log on to the Science Network Web site: Beyond Belief: "Science, Religion, Reason and Survival," http://beyondbelief2006.org.
5. Johnson, "A Free-for-All on Science and Religion."
6. Ibid.
7. This plot synopsis was taken from the scripts for "Go God Go," Episodes 1012 and 1013 of *South Park*, http://www.tv.com/south-park/show/344/episode.html (see Season 10).
8. See "Would Freezing Ted Williams Really Work?" *ABC News*, http://abcnews.go.com/US/story?id=91481&page=1.
9. "Go God Go," Episode 1013.
10. "Go God Go," Episode 1012.
11. "Go God Go," Episode 1013.
12. See Daniel Sorrell, "South Park Takes On Richard Dawkins, *The Revealer*, November 20, 2006, http://www.therevealer.org/archives/timeless_002719.php.
13. Rollins, "Creationism Is Scientific," *Ignite* blog, January 21, 2007, http://www.ignite.cd/blogs/Pete/index.cfm?postid=613.
14. Ann Coulter, *Godless: The Church of Liberalism* (New York: Crown Forum, 2006).
15. For an in-depth analysis of the religious themes present in *South Park*, see Becky Garrison, "The Search for the Historical Kenny," *The Wittenburg Door*, January/February 2002.
16. "Go God Go," Episode 1012.
17. Plantinga, "The Dawkins Confusion."
18. Kenneth R. Miller, *Finding Darwin's God* (New York: Harper Collins, 1999), 291. Reprinted by permission of HarperCollins Publishers.
19. Wolpert, *Six Impossible Things*, 212–13.
20. See Plantinga, "The Dawkins Confusion."

21. Jörg Blech and Johann Grolle, "Darwinism Completely Refutes Intelligent Design" originally published in *Der Spiegel* 52/2005, 143ff.

22. "John Howland and Elizabeth Tilly," http://www.boydhouse.com/michelle/gorham/johnhowland.html.

23. See Johnson, "A Free-for-All on Science and Religion."

24. Roughgarden, *Evolution and Christian Faith*, 17.

25. Collins, *The Language of God*, 205.

26. See Day and Scott, *Praying in the Presence of Our Lord*.

27. See Becky Garrison, "Water Talk," *Flyfish.com*, March 19, 2004, http://www.flyfish.com/newsroom/editorial.php?id=224&Fly_Session=830ca3d942c985e86d6ee593cf401c75.

28. Collins, *The Language of God*, 165.

29. McGrath, *The Twilight of Atheism*, 109.

30. Collins, *The Language of God*, 165.

31. For additional information about Charles Darwin's faith journey, check out William E. Phipps, *Darwin's Religious Odyssey* (Philadelphia, PA: Trinity Press International, 2002).

32. David Sloan Wilson, *Evolution Is for Everyone* (New York: Delacorte Press, 2007), 6.

33. Steven Wright, *The Funny Pages* (Kansas City, MO: Andrews McMeel, 2002), 88.

34. See Dawkins, *The God Delusion*, 77–81.

35. Collins, *The Language of God*, 153.

36. Jeanine K. Brown, *Scripture as Communication* (Grand Rapids, MI: Baker Books, 2007), 34.

37. For those wishing to delve into twenty-first-century biblical scholarship, check out N. T. Wright, *The Last Word: Beyond the Bible Wars to a New Understanding of the Authority of Scripture* (San Francisco: HarperSanFrancisco, 2005) for a very good introduction to the topic.

38. N. T. Wright, *Simply Christian: Why Christianity Makes Sense* (San Francisco: HarperSanFrancisco, 2006), 182. Reprinted by permission of HarperCollins Publishers.

39. Simon Calloway Morris, interview by Emily Winslow Stark, *The Wittenburg Door*, March/April 2007.

40. Miller, *Finding Darwin's God*, 167.

NOTES

41. *Life: How Did It Get Here? By Evolution or by Creation?* (Brooklyn, NY: Watch Tower Bible and Tract Society of Pennsylvania, 1985).

42. Caputo, *Philosophy and Theology*, 8.

43. Sam Harris, "The Politics of Ignorance," *The Huffington Post*, August 2, 2005, http://www.huffingtonpost.com/sam-harris/the-politics-of-ignorance_b_5053.html. Note: The scientists I am quoting in this chapter are considered tops in their respective fields. I have deliberately shied away from the controversial creationist journals and their atheist counterparts. I don't want to sift through shoddy scholarship any more than the next sane soul. But I would encourage those reading Dawkins, Harris, and Dennett to also pick up Collins, Miller, and Roughgarden so we can start to dialogue. I'm sick of this dirty dissin'.

44. Segal, "Atheist Evangelist."

45. See Wolpert, *Six Impossible Things*, for starters.

46. St. Augustine, *The Confessions of St. Augustine*, Book One, chap. 1, paragraph 1.

47. Roughgarden, *Evolution and Christian Faith*, 129

48. Ibid., 132–33.

49. Ibid., 133.

50. Ibid., 128–29.

51. Ibid., 127.

52. Ibid.

53. Ibid.

54. See 1 Corinthians 12:1–31.

55. 1 Cor. 12:20.

56. 1 Cor. 12:12.

57. Roughgarden, *Evolution and Christian Faith*, 19.

PHYSICIAN, HEAL THYSELF

1. "God Debate: Sam Harris vs. Rick Warren."

2. Garrison, *Red and Blue God, Black and Blue Church*, 87-98.

3. Collins, *The Language of God*, 257.

4. Harris, *Letter to a Christian Nation*, 38.

5. Dawkins, *The God Delusion*, 295–97.

6. Flip Benham, interview by Becky Garrison, *The Wittenburg Door*, September/October 2000. Note: Operation Save America used to be

called Operation Rescue during those wild crazy abortion clinic demonstration days. After catching too much flak for their follies, I guess they decided to clean up their image with a more family friendly-name change when the demonstrations turned deadly.

7. Collins, *The Language of God*, 211.

8. Ibid., 243–44.

9. Joan Roughgarden, "Beyond Belief 2006: Science, Religion, Reason and Survival," Session 3.

10. Collins, *The Language of God*, 272.

11. Jörg Blech, "Researchers Crusade Against American Fundamentalists," originally published in *Der Spiegel* 43/2006,188ff.

12. For a succinct analysis of the role of religion in stem cell research, see Dan Gilgoff, "Religious Right Takes on Stem Cell Research," *US News & World Report*, July 18, 2006, http://www.usnews.com/usnews/news/articles/060718/18stemcell.htm.

13. "Interview: Sam Harris," *Religion & Ethics Newsweekly*, Episode no. 1019, January 5, 2007, http://www.pbs.org/wnet/religionandethics/week1019/interview2.html. Courtesy Religion & Ethics Newsweekly. Thirteen/WNET, New York.

14. "Profile: Dr. Francis Collins," *Religion & Ethics Newsweekly*, July 21, 2006, episode No. 947, http://www.pbs.org/wnet/religionandethics/week947/profile.html. Courtesy Religion & Ethics Newsweekly. Thirteen/WNET, New York.

15. Gilgoff highlights the potential political fallout for those Republicans who chose to go against the wishes of select Religious Right activists.

16. See Garrison, *Red and Blue God, Black and Blue Church*, 87.

17. Jim Wallis, "Voting God's Politics," God's Politics Blog, November 3, 2006, http://www.beliefnet.com/blogs/godspolitics/2006/11/jim-wallis-voting-gods-politics.html. © Sojourners 2007. This article appeared originally on www.beliefnet.com, the leading website for faith, spirituality, inspiration & more. Used with permission. All rights reserved.

18. Dawkins, "Collateral Damage 1: Embryos and Stem Cell Research," *Science: In the News*, August 1, 2006, http://richarddawkins.net/article,157,Collateral-Damage-1-Embryos-and-Stem-Cell-Research,Richard-Dawkins.

19. As I reported in *Red and Blue God, Black and Blue Church*, according to the *American Journal of Medicine*, health care lobbyists spent $237 million—

more than any other industry—to influence U.S. senators and represen-
tatives, the White House, and federal agencies in 2000, an election
year. See Janice Hopkins Tanne, "U.S. Healthcare Lobbyists Outspend
Other Pressure Groups," *BMJ* 328 (April 3, 2004), 786, and credited to
the *American Journal of Medicine* 116 (2004), 474–77

20. Sarah Kliff, "Golden Eggs: When Donation Funds an Education,"
    Current, Summer 2006, http://www.msnbc.msn.com/
    id/12209274/site/newsweek.

21. See Garrison, *Swamp*, 93–94.

22. Stanley Hauerwas, *Connecticut Medicine*, 39:815-17, 1975.

23. John F. Kavanaugh, "Food for Terri Schiavo," *America*, November 24,
    2003, http://www.americamagazine.org/gettext.cfm?textID=
    3296&articleTypeID=7&issueID=461

24. Garrison, *Swamp*.

25. David Shore as quoted in "God No!" *On the Media* (New York Public
    Radio), August 17, 2007.

26. For those of you who aren't addicted to TV medical dramas, a code is
    called when the heart stops beating. A crew of doctors and nurses con-
    verge on the patient to try to jump-start the heart so it can start pump-
    ing either on its own or through the use of machines. Fortunately, I
    have a strong stomach or else I would have turned a rather undignified
    shade of green, and my ability to serve as a prayerful presence would
    have become more than a bit puke-y.

27. I do recall catching some heat for doing these sacramental moves. A
    fellow chaplain intern from a Pentecostal background told me I'd burn
    in hell for blessing the dead. Also, one of the Catholic chaplain interns
    asked me what the body temperature of the infants was. According to
    his rulebook, for the baptism to "take," the flesh had to be warm. My
    stance was that I wasn't there for the infant's soul but there to provide
    consolation to the mother. But all these dudes around me seemed to
    care about was whether or not I broke some man-made rule. Now you
    see why I became a satirist. Humor is the saving grace that keeps me
    from becoming an atheist.

28. "Study of the Therapeutic Effects of Intercessory Prayer (STEP)," the
    John Templeton Foundation Web site, http://www.templeton.org/
    newsroom/press_releases/060407step.html.

29. "Loneliness Could Boost Alzheimer's Risk," *HealthDay News*, February 7, 2007, http://health.yahoo.com/news/171700.
30. From *Man's Search for Meaning* by Viktor E. Frankl. Copyright © 1959, 1962, 1984, 1992 by Viktor E. Frankl. Reprinted by permission of Beacon Press, Boston.

RAPTURE READY?

1. Blech and Grolle, "Darwinism Completely Refutes Intelligent Design."
2. Jason Boyett, *The Pocket Guide to the Apocalypse: The Official Field Manual for the End of the World* (Orlando, FL: Relevant Books, 2005).
3. If you want to get the full flavor of how I feel about this mess, check out my interview with Todd Strandberg, coauthor of *Are You Rapture Ready?*, *The Wittenberg Door*, May/June 2004, http://wittenburgdoor.com/archives/toddstrandberg.html.
4. See Campolo, *Letters to a Young Evangelical*, 107.
5. See Matthew 5–7 NKJV
6. Richard Kearney, "Thinking after Terror: An Interreligious Challenge," *Journal of the Interdisciplinary Crossroads* 2, no. 1 (April 2005), 14.
7. Ibid., 18.
8. August Berkshire, vice president of Atheist Alliance International, as quoted by Hemant Mehta, "18 Unconvincing Arguments for God," January 25, 2007, http://friendlyatheist.com/2007/01/25/18-unconvincing-arguments-for-god.
9. Harris, "Why Are Atheists So Angry?"
10. Harris, *The End of Faith*, 15.
11. Bethanne Patrick, "License to Be Bold," AOL Books Web site, http://books.aol.com/feature/_a/license-to-be-bold/20060717101109990001.
12. Wilberforce, *Real Christianity*, 22.
13. Jerry Jenkins, interview by Becky Garrison, *The Wittenberg Door*, March/April 2005.
14. See Matthew 28:18.
15. Sam Harris, "A Dissent: The Case Against Faith," *Newsweek* Nov. 13, 2006.
16. See Barbara Rossing, *The Rapture Exposed* (Boulder, CO: Westview Press, 2005), 8.

17. Garrison, "Re-evaluating the Rapture," God's Politics blog, February 16, 2007, http://blog.beliefnet.com/godspolitics/2007/02/becky-garrison-re-evaluating-rapture.html. This article appeared originally on www.beliefnet.com, the leading website for faith, spirituality, inspiration & more. Used with permission. All rights reserved.

18. McLaren, *The Secret Message of Jesus*, 23.

19. Stephen Shoemaker, *Being Christian in an Almost Chosen Nation* (Nashville: Abingdon Press), 113; see Luke 12:2–3.

20. Edward O. Wilson, *The Creation: An Appeal to Save Life on Earth* (New York: W. W. Norton & Co., 2006), 5.

21. See McLaren, "Joseph, Noah, and Pre-emptive Preservation," *God's Politics*, March 12, 2007, http://www.beliefnet.com/blogs/godspolitics/2007/03/brian-mclaren-joseph-noah-and-pre.html. This article appeared originally on www.beliefnet.com, the leading website for faith, spirituality, inspiration & more. Used with permission. All rights reserved.

22. Wilson, *Creation*, 167.

23. "Atheists Split over Message," *Beliefnet*, March 30, 2007, http://www.beliefnet.com/story/215/story_21519_1.html (as accessed on April 23, 2007). This article appeared originally on www.beliefnet.com, the leading website for faith, spirituality, inspiration & more. Used with permission. All rights reserved.

24. Ibid.

25. Simon Hooper, "The Rise of the New Atheists," *CNN.com*, http://www.cnn.com/2006/WORLD/europe/11/08/atheism.feature/index.html.

26. Paul Kurtz, "Are 'Evangelical Atheists' Too Outspoken?" Council for Secular Humanism Web site, http://www.secularhumanism.org/index.php?section=library&page=kurtz_27_2.

27. McGrath and Collicut McGrath, *The Dawkins Delusion*, 21.

28. Helen Mildenhall, personal e-mail (March 10, 2007). For more information about "Off The Map," log on to http://www.off-the-map.org.

WALKING THE WALK

1. Dawkins, *The God Delusion*, 253.

2. Jonathan Luxmoore, "The Dawkins Delusion: Britain's Crusading Atheist," *Commonweal*, April 20, 2007, http://www.commonwealmagazine.org/article.php3?id_article=1914 (as accessed on May 8, 2007).

3. See Genesis 19:26.

4. See "Gay Tinky Winky Bad for Children," *BBC*, February 15, 1999, http://news.bbc.co.uk/1/hi/entertainment/276677.stm (as accessed April 22, 2007).

5. See Matthew 22:36–40

6. Some days I can laugh off the garbage that goes with being a chick in this whole religious-publishing biz. But if I'm particularly cranky and stressed out, certain goateed guys can really get my goat.

7. Yaconelli, "Reflections."

8. Nadia Bolz-Weber, "The Problem with Christian Love," the Sarcastic Lutheran Web site, April 12, 2007, http://sarcasticlutheran.typepad.com/sarcastic_lutheran/2007/04/the_problem_wit.html.

9. Ibid.

10. Wright, *Simply Christian*, 187.

11 McLaren, *The Secret Message of Jesus*, 83.

12 See "The Lutheran World Relief Fair Trade Coffee Project," http://www.lwr.org/coffee/index.asp, for one example of how churches can provide coffee that is good for the soul as well as the palate.

13. McLaren, *The Secret Message of Jesus*, 31.

14. See Matthew 19:24 for the actual verse upon which this admittedly flip biblical interpretation is based.

15. See Garrison, "Jesus Died for THIS?"

16. E. J. Dionne Jr., "Answers to the Atheists," *Washington Post*, April 6, 2007; A21, http://www.washingtonpost.com/wp-dyn/content/article/2007/04/05/AR2007040501790.html.

17. John 3:16 NKJV.

18. See Garrison, "Jesus Died for THIS?"

19. Fox, *Jesus in America*, 406. Reprinted by permission of Harper Collins Publishers.

20. Jim Wallis, *The Call to Conversion*, rev. and upd. ed. (San Francisco: HarperSanFrancisco, 2005), 22.

21. See Hooper, "Rise of the New Atheists."

22. Harris, *Letter to a Christian Nation*, 43.

23. See their Web site at http://www.gordonconwell.edu/ockenga/globalchristianity; Wolf Simson, personal e-mail, February 27, 2007.

24. Simson, *Fridayfax* 2, Issue #2, January 2007, http://www.english.ffax2.com.

25. Simson, personal e-mail, February 27, 2007.

26. Sites Unseen Web page: http://zoecarnate.com.

27. Mike Morrell, personal e-mail, April 22, 2007.

28. Cheryl Lawrie, personal e-mail, June 25, 2007.

29. McLaren, *Secret Message of Jesus*, 83.

30. "The Future of the Emerging Church," *Christianity Today*, March 19, 2007, http://blog.christianitytoday.com/outofur/archives/2007/03/the_future_of_t.html). Note: It is not within the scope of this book to elaborate on the nuances of the emerging church. Also, I'm a satirist not a theologian, sociologist or philosopher. So, I will defer to those with more specialized training to comment on this admittedly controversial movement. For those desiring a quick overview of the emerging church, check out Scot McKnight, "Five Streams of the Emerging Church," *Christianity Today*, January 19, 2007, http://www.christianitytoday.com/40534.

31. Ibid.

32. See Rob Lacey, interview by Becky Garrison, *The Wittenburg Door*, March/April 2006.

33. Tickle, *The Words of Jesus: A Gospel of the Sayings of Our Lord with Reflections by Phyllis Tickle*. (San Francisco: Jossey-Bass, 2008), 84–85.

34. Lacey, *The Liberator* (Grand Rapids, MI: Zondervan, 2006); *Inspired by the Bible Experience: New Testament (CD)* (Grand Rapids, MI: Zondervan, 2006).

35. Rollins, *How (Not) to Speak of God*, 22.

36. http://www.sanctuaryny.org/blog.

37. See Amy Zimmer, "The Way, the Truth and the Limelight," April 9, 2007, http://www.tracyquan.net/MetroEaster.pdf.

38. Kester Brewin, "[Grid::Blog::Via Crucis 2007] It's Not the Winning That Matters, It's . . . | The End of Strategy [5]," *Signs of Emergence* Web page, http://kester.typepad.com/signs/2007/04/gridblogvia_cru_4.html.

39. Yaconelli, "Reflections."

40. See John 2:1–11; Luke 5:38.

Notes

Epilogue

1. "The Nightline Face-Off: Christians and Atheists to Debate the Existence of God," *ABC News*, May 2, 2007, http://abcnews.go.com/Nightline/story?id=3130360&page=1&CMP=OTC-RSSFeeds0312.
2. See "4 Prodigies, Nobelists and Penguins: Science and Stereotypes in the Movies," http://www.tribecafilmfestival.org/tff-ep-tribeca-talks/html.
3. See Garrison, "Christian vs. Atheist Celebrity Death Match."

Appendix A: Select Dates in New Atheist History

1. Portions of this timeline appeared in *Red and Blue God, Black and Blue Church*, 143–50. For those desiring a fun romp through Christian history check out Stephen Tomkins, *A Short History of Christianity*.

Appendix B: Interview with Hemant a.k.a. The Friendly Atheist

1. See http://www.friendlyatheist.com and Hemant Mehta, *I Sold My Soul on eBay* (New York: WaterBrook Press, 2007).

ABOUT THE AUTHOR

BECKY GARRISON serves as Senior Contributing Editor for *The Wittenburg Door*, the oldest, largest, and only religious satire magazine in the United States. Her additional writing credits include work for *The New York Times*, *The Tonight Show*, *Christian Retailing, and* Relevantmagazine.com. Garrison also contributes to *The Ooze* and blogs on *God's Politics*. She has a dual Master of Divinity/Social Work degree from Yale University and Columbia University, and an undergraduate degree in theater arts from Wake Forest University.